What Others Are Saying...

I really like Lynn Hoover's approach and common sense ideas in this book, and her use of case studies to make her points. I think readers will get a lot out of seeing examples of the points she is making about real-life situations.

Lynn really gets to the heart of recognizing behavior problems as miscommunication between species. She identifies how fear and anxiety factor into many of the behavior problems we deal with. The understanding of the need to alter the animal's environment and the owner's interactions so as to not trigger or give pets the ability to engage in problem behaviors is essential to therapy, and she states this strongly in several areas of the book. She also emphasizes redirection to more appropriate behaviors and the principles of positive reinforcement.

Under "Who Qualifies", my basic tenet is the veterinarian needs to be involved at the outset to rule out medical issues and then make the proper referral. It should be the veterinarian who coordinates this. I think the way Lynn represents the veterinarian's role is accurate and honest. She makes a point to stress the need for veterinary evaluation of problems and also defers to the veterinarian when it comes to the use of medications. However, she rightly states that it is up to pet's owners to educate themselves in order to best be involved in the decision making process.

I, of course, agree with Lynn's position on the fallacy of dominance theory. Lynn's passion comes across to the reader. I hope the book sells well. It can only hope to advance the cause of positive dog training and encourage people to get help when it comes to more problematic behaviors.

~ John Ciribassi, DVM, Dipl. ACVB
Past President, American Veterinary Society of Animal Behavior (AVSAB)
Chicagoland Veterinary Behavior Consultants
www.chicagovetbehavior.com

"Lynn's explanations of dog behavior and solutions in the "Case Histories" section are an education for anyone looking for realistic and reliable solutions for "dog quirks," as she so charmingly categorizes dog problems. It is wonderful to have someone with Lynn's insight to guide us.

I first met Lynn when she had taken on the task of creating a place for animal behavior professionals to get continuing education and certification. As I talked with Lynn, I was taken by her philosophy and vision: the combination of the dream and the where-with-all to make something of it. When I was able to meet Lynn in person, what struck me first was her kind nature which is finding a voice in her commitment to helping dogs and people have better lives—something I have also devoted my life's work to. It is always so very pleasing and validating to know someone who can articulate those points that are near and dear to our hearts.

I love this book. It will have a prominent place on my bookshelf - to be used as reference, inspiration and to be lent to those whom I am certain will return it to me! Lynn tackles tough subjects that face animal professionals in current times and does so in a logical and professional manner, with honesty. Her message of a professional attitude, tolerance and ethics is an important one.

~ Brenda Aloff
Author of, *Aggression in Dogs: Practical Management, Prevention and Behavior Modification*, and
Get Connected with Your Dog: Emphasizing the Relationship While Training Your Dog, and
Canine Body Language: A Photographic Guide Interpreting the Native Language of the Domestic Dog
www.brendaaloff.com
Midland, MI

"Lynn Hoover's insights and her recommendations for managing canine behaviors are based squarely on scientific research, loving observation, and a joyful appreciation of dogs and the bonds between our two species. If you want to live happily ever after with your dog, read *Dog Quirks*."

~ Sheila Webster Boneham, PhD, Author of
Rescue Matters! How to Find, Foster, and Rehome Companion Animals, and
Training Your Dog for Life

"Lots of practical advice and methods for solving dog behavior problems. This book is especially recommended for people who work with dog behavior problems that are caused by either separation anxiety or fear."

~ Temple Grandin, PhD
Author of, *Animals in Translation,* and
Animals Make us Human

"I really like the book and want people to read it. Lynn Hoover is a fine writer. Her work always has an immediacy and personalism so the reader feels they're right there in the room. I love Section Two, "All That Matters". So much wisdom and insight in those chapters. I like the "Case Studies" a lot. Lynn opens a window for the reader into her philosophy, methodology, and style. I like the idea of the Behavior Cache --- brief essays on assorted important but often little-discussed topics, along with excellent references for readers who want to know more."

~ Dani Weinberg, PhD
Dogs & Their People
Karen Pryor Academy Faculty
Author of, *Teaching People Teaching Dogs*
Albuquerque, NM

What Others Are Saying...

"Reading this book was like sitting down with a dear friend. The advice is genuine and after completing it, you feel sad it's over...

The true measure of a book's worth is, simply, did it make you think after reading it. Lynn makes one think. It has not been since Clothier's *Bones* that I was moved by case studies. Great job, Lynn."

~ Carol Stewart, MA, CPDT
Certified Pet Dog Trainer
Greensburg, PA

"I started reading *Dog Quirks And Behavior Solutions* on a trip. I was so captivated I stayed in my room and ordered room service until I finished it. When I got home I hugged my quirky dog and promised her I'd be there for her."

~ Nancy Davis, MA
Buffalo, NY

"Beautifully written...insightful...empowering!"

~ Peter Smith, MA.
Pittsburgh, PA

Dog Quirks

And Behavior Solutions

Lynn Hoover

DOG QUIRKS AND BEHAVIOR SOLUTIONS
Copyright ©2010 Lynn Hoover

Limits of Liability and Disclaimer of Warranty:

Consulting Editor: Rebecca Hoover
Substantive Editor: Joanne Hirase-Stacey

Publisher's Cataloging-in-Publication Data

    Hoover, Lynn D.
    Dog quirks and behavior solutions / Lynn Hoover.
    p. cm.
    Includes bibliographical references and index.
    ISBN 978-0-9779949-4-6
1. Dogs – Training. 2. Dogs – Behavior. I. Title.

SF431 .H7935 2010
636.7/0887—dc22   LCCN: 2010921496

Published by Dog Quirks LLC - Pittsburgh, PA

To Jim

Who makes all things possible

Table of Contents

Acknowledgments

Very special thanks to my husband, Jim, for standing by me when I wrote this. Thanks to my daughter, Rebecca, for her keen insight and enthusiastic support, and my son, Jeff, for his incredible wit and essential wisdom. Thanks to all my family for their endless reservoir of love.

I'd also like to thank:

Dr. Dani Weinberg and Dr. John Ciribassi for their invaluable and insightful feedback that resulted in significant improvement to my manuscript; also, for their qualities of integrity, professionalism and commitment to excellence.

Niki Lamproplos, Carole Duffy, Michelle Douglas, Brenda Aloff, and Morgan Spector, for their support and invaluable contributions, strong ethics, and commitment to bringing about positive outcomes for dogs and their families.

Leonard Press for modeling professionalism, authenticity and flawless integrity all these years.

My terrific editor, Joanne Hirase-Stacey of Readable Writer, for her uncommonly good advice. Readers can find her at www.readablewriter.com.

My client families who gave their stories so others would benefit, and the Pleasant Hills Library Writer's Group, for their early guidance and for getting me past many writer's blocks.

All the committed behaviorists, behavior consultants and trainers out there who understand, the truth has to matter and positive regard is the heart of professionalism.

SECTION ONE

DOGS
WITH ISSUES

Introduction

I'm driving to a consult with a family that has endured expensive trips to the animal emergency hospital with their Airedale. Ali eats pencils, rocks, lipsticks and socks that can't make their way through his digestive system without medical assistance. Veterinarians have tagged him as having an obsessive-compulsive disorder, eating disorder, pica, pathological anxiety, and a perpetual irritable bowel. The family's embarrassed and wonders how they've contributed to his living so neurotically. They've tried "everything" to stop him but he grows more proficient as a thief and tasteless glutton (with tummy aches). What will it take to divert Ali from eating in such an original way?

Later, as I'm driving back to my office from my visit with Ali, I spot a young woman, yanking on the leash of a Labrador retriever who is trying desperately to get in some good sniffs, presumably before being forced to head home. The woman issues a command, "Let's go!" but the dog seems to have forgotten his obedience training on this day. Should she impose her will on him or let him have his way?

We'll revisit Ali and his unusual eating habits in the "Behavior Cache" section towards the end of the book (p. 165). If you proceed through the chapters in an orderly fashion, by the time you encounter "Ali the Airedale Update" you'll likely understand the strategies I employed and how they led to a reasonably successful outcome.

But let's return for the moment to our Labrador retriever who persists at sniffing when his person wants to move on. We might surmise he wants to stay with scents long enough to determine what movement took place there. He wants to know who passed through and where they've gone. Families are typically not interested in this type of information and some undoubtedly consider their dog's pursuits pointless. I think we can agree that when humans snoop on neighbors they are a lot more discreet about it.

Dogs have a highly refined sense of smell; their abilities are vastly superior to ours. Most dogs enjoy using their noses to discern Who's Who in their neighborhoods. You might not be impressed with this fact, but whereas we humans can sometimes smell pee, dogs know with certainty who left it and can figure out if they are long gone or just around the corner!

"So what?" you ask. "Yuck!" Well, if you taught your dogs to track, you could participate in lost dog searches. A lot of dogs get lost and our dogs would be a whole lot better at finding them than we are.

Linda Case of AutumnGold Consulting in central Illinois and an instructor for the College of Veterinary Medicine at the University of Illinois, wrote in her 2005 book, *The Dog: Its Behavior, Nutrition, and Health*, "The olfactory acuity of the domestic dog is well documented, and odors play an enormous role in many aspects of canine behavior… A good way to appreciate the importance of scent to the dog is to imagine that the dog perceives his world through 'nose pictures'. By comparison, humans are woefully inadequate in scenting ability."[1]

Moreover, researchers estimate dogs have between 220 million[2] and 2 billion[3] olfactory neurons in the olfactory epithelium of the nose. Humans, in contrast, have only about 5 million. Behavior experiments that focus on a dog's ability to detect the presence of an odor in contrast to humans have shown that "dogs have 100 to 1000 times the ability of humans."[4]

We know dogs pack awesome power in their noses and yet it takes time, energy and commitment to teach dogs to use their innate abilities in a disciplined way, more than it takes to modify most problem behaviors. Neverthe-

1   Case, Linda P. *The Dog: Its Behavior, Nutrition, and Health*. (Blackwell Publishing ltd., 2005) 55.

2   A. Schoon. "The Performance of Dogs in Identifying Humans by Scent." (Ph.D. dissertation, Rijks-univeristeit, Leiden), 1997. Citing Droscher.

3   D.G. Moulton, "Minimum odorant concentrations detectable by the dog and their implications for olfactory receptor sensitivity," in *Chemical Signals in Vertebrates,* eds. Dietland Muller-Schwarze, and Robert M Silverstein. (New York: Plenum Press, 1977), 455-64.

4   A. Schoon, "The Performance of Dogs in Identifying Humans by Scent".

less, tracking does provide a great diversion for some misbehavin' dogs that are bored and need a fun job to keep them out of trouble.

Let's look at another bright side to this scenario with the Labrador and other dogs that are serious about sniffing. We don't have to take our sniffer-dogs to the Grand Canyon or Niagara Falls to elicit intense interest in their environment. A trip to the mailbox or a corner telephone pole usually provides entertainment enough. It goes without saying that dogs are easier to please than children and in-laws in this regard.

Now let's imagine our Labrador has major issues: he puts on big aggressive displays for the dogs in his neighborhood. When he's out and about with his family, he growls ferociously while straining at the end of his leash and lunging at every within-range dog. His people are understandably embarrassed and want to head straight for home. To onlookers, it appears as if the Labrador is enjoying himself immensely.

Who knows, they might be partially right. Our seemingly fearless Labrador could communicate with his dog-quarry in dog language, something to the effect of "roll over now or we're gonna' kick your butt!" Notice he says "we". With his person at the other end of the leash he might conclude that they're on the same team. He might even imagine she's proud of his hard-won standing in the 'hood. If he were all alone out there he certainly wouldn't carry on with such apparent confidence.

Some scientific types will surely complain that it's wrong to anthropomorphize by suggesting warrior dogs entertain themselves with their bravado, put on a show for others, and are driven by emotions. These individuals believe it is erroneous to attribute human motivations, characteristics, feelings, or behaviors to dogs. They advise that we ought to stick to describing behavior and skip the empathy for our furry friends. Empathy takes animal observers down the wrong path, some would say.

I have long been intrigued by the narrowness of this view, more so when the scientists are technically correct but functionally unhelpful. Why deny that dogs have feelings, drives and motivations, even if we don't know exactly what they are, unless it can be established that such recognition results in harm or thwarts problem-solving?

Empathy is about understanding, being aware of, being sensitive to, and vicariously experiencing the feelings, thoughts, and experiences of others. While dogs undoubtedly do suffer from misunderstanding caused by owner anthropomorphizing, they surely suffer as acutely when their humans fail to empathize with them, draw the wrong conclusions about their motivations and needs, and derail relationships.

As an animal behavior consultant, it's my job to figure out how to manage and modify a broad mix of worrisome behaviors and motivate families to follow my lead. Empathy is my guide. The central issue for me is that empathy makes deep emotional connections between animals and humans possible, and sensitizes us to their needs. Such sensitization helps us form loving bonds with dogs, who more likely "think in pictures", as posited by Dr. Temple Grandin in *Animals Make Us Human*[5], and not necessarily as I sometimes humorously portray dog's thought processes when I'm hot on the path to helping them change.

Humans are capable of forming deep, empathic bonds with dogs and dogs nourish us with their attentive devotion in return. We are the ones most responsible for meeting dog's needs. With all the problematic behavior we see in companion dogs we can rightfully ask, "Are today's families capable of meeting their dog's needs as well as past generations?" and, "When confronted with dogs with issues, are the solutions families select apt to help their dogs or harm them?"

Some needs are being met better today and others are not. For example, today's dogs generally have access to temperature-controlled rooms to give them respite from searing heat and bitter cold; however, they usually aren't as free to run around, or to follow scents and play in their own way. They can't make the rounds in neighborhoods to collect biscuits and extend their network of friends. Energetic young dogs are being confined to crates all day to keep them "safe" while their families work.

Some families are tuned in to their dog's natural inclinations and amused by their enthusiasms. Other families try to shape their dogs into something dif-

....

5   Temple Grandin, PhD and Catherine Johnson PhD. *Animals Make Us Human: Creating the Best Life for Animals.*(Mariner Books,2010).

ferent than what they are, and different from what they can be, even on their best days. With each family I encounter in a consulting relationship, I show them how to bring out the best in their dogs and narrow gulfs of misunderstanding between the species.

Americans are typically ambivalent about their dogs. On the one hand, we invite dogs into our homes and hearts and love them with a bond that is like none other. On the other hand, we fear the obligations if our feelings for them run too deep.

If dogs become sick, where do we draw the line between paying for expensive veterinary care and meeting the cost of family necessities? If misbehaving dogs detract from the quality of life for families, to what extent should families extend themselves to aid in their dog's reformations?

Sometimes my clients talk about their dogs in disparaging terms. Stressed, they refer to their canine companion as "just a dog" or threaten, "We might have to get rid of the dog." If dogs are truly this dispensable, why do these owners grieve so when they lose one?

I work almost exclusively with dogs whose behaviors put them at risk of being misunderstood, inappropriately punished, discarded, and even euthanized. Some examples are those dogs that wreck the house when their owners are out, or growl menacingly at visitors. With a reliable assessment, a good plan, and a committed, energetic family, most of these dogs can be settled in with their families in more acceptable ways.

My job is to recognize what individual dogs need to be happy and balanced. To succeed, I must discern the best reinforcers for each animal so I can offer them as rewards for "good" behavior. Reinforcers are used to "increase the probability that the preceding response will occur in the future".[6]

Treats, belly rubs and chase games are examples of positive reinforcers that appeal to dogs. If you reward the behaviors you want, your dog will repeat those "good" behaviors to get more rewards. When you inadvertently reward behaviors you don't want, dogs similarly repeat the "bad" behaviors to get rewards. It's that simple. From your dog's perspective, any behavior that brings

---

6   Charles Morris. *Psychology: An Introduction.* (Prentice Hall, 7th ed., 1990), 188.

rewards is "good" behavior.

With empathy for all, and an eye on reinforcers that meet dog's real-time needs, I'll tell you stories about some of the dogs I've known, their individual quirks, and the families that live with them. Most families invited me to their homes to do formal consults and I appreciate this opportunity to share their stories with you. During the process, I'll reveal some of my own story because you need to know who I am to understand my philosophy and techniques.

This book is for families, behaviorists, trainers, behavior consultants, rescue workers, veterinarians, and others who want to make sound choices and be there in a meaningful way for the dogs in their care. The information I set forth is reliable and, when available, backed by research. My overarching goal is for you to see how I go from empathy and accurate assessment of need, to action, and how you too can make it interesting and enjoyable for your dogs to learn new behaviors and thrive in their families and communities.

Many dogs have behavior problems that can be remedied using simple sets of interventions. The families most likely to succeed are the ones open to viewing their dogs in novel ways and using reinforcers creatively to shape more desirable behaviors.

There's nothing unusual about the families whose stories are told here. They are just like us. At times, they are us: not the only cause of our dogs' difficulties, but as we know, dogs have quirks and there's room for improvement in any relationship. Families can be powerful instruments for change: to elicit different, "healthier" responses, families have to change how they interact with their dogs.

The dogs in these chapters have their share of problems: separation distress, aggression in various forms, elimination in the wrong places, debilitating shyness, obvious anxiety, anxiety cloaked as bravado. With these stories, I will share with you simple truths about dogs and our relationships with them.

A couple of cases are very long and detailed; others are short vignettes. I'll illustrate in many different ways the basic principles and techniques I use to successfully reshape dog behavior and avoid causing harm. I refer to research often enough to reassure you that I have not gone too far astray with anthropomorphisms and appeals to dog's emotions. I hope you find my methods simple and easy to employ, flexible, and non-doctrinaire. Please don't try to cherry-pick your way through the book. It's meant to be taken as a whole with the whole greater than the sum total of its parts.

Let's have fun with all of this. If we were discussing children with psychiatric disorders, we would be suitably serious. But living and working with dogs is a whole lot easier, in part because we can be lighthearted about them. So let's loosen up; dogs are funny and figuring out how to get them to do things our way can be fun for them and us too.

With a can-do spirit, we can help a whole lot of at-risk dogs and their families who might think they have no choice but to give up on them. Yes, we surely can!

Lifelines

It's mid-winter as I write this. We've had a few days respite from bitter cold and the ice in the lakes and harbors is melting. I keep an eye on the news as I mull over ideas. Out there in an ice-filled harbor in Massachusetts, 200 feet from shore, trapped amid the ice floes, is Olly, a black Labrador retriever. While chasing after some geese, he fell in and couldn't extricate himself. But Olly wasn't left to his doom. Three firefighters in wet suits ventured into the frigid water to pull Olly to safety. A larger contingency of firefighters is onshore, securing the rescue of the dog and their comrades.

The ice is thick and the lead firefighter, Jim Sheard of the Hingham Fire Department, couldn't initially reach Olly. Sheard called to the dog, "Come on buddy, come on, you got to give me a hand." Talking about the incident afterward, he said the exhausted Olly "actually had enough energy to come toward me." The two connected and, with support from the other firefighters, they were reeled in to shore. Sheard said, "Dogs definitely have a sense that you are there to help."[1]

On shore, Olly's family waited for him with warm blankets. The father scooped up the exhausted dog and rushed him to his car and on to a veterinary hospital, where he was proclaimed healthy in spite of his ordeal. Olly

----

[1]   "Firefighters Rescue Dog From Icy Waters", *2009 Sunbeam Television Corp.* Feb. 6, 2009.

was going to be okay, thanks to the Americans who cared.

The family and the firefighters could have said "he's just a dog" and left him to a horrible fate, but that's not how we like to do things in America.

The misbehaving dogs I encounter in my practice are ensnared in ice floes like Olly, not physically, but emotionally. Some look around and see danger everywhere. They don't understand that if they bite the hand that feeds them, their lives might end. If they pee too persistently in the house, they may be sent to a backyard to live out their days, all alone, or packed off to a shelter, divorced from their family. If they wreck things when their owners are away because they're frantic over being left home alone, their humans might withdraw love, food and shelter—everything that gave the dog a sense of security.

If you're reading this book, chances are you're willing to gear up like the firefighters for your dogs with issues, and meet them with a lifeline. I hope you'll join me in saying to troubled dogs, "Come on buddy, come on, you got to give me a hand". Perhaps they will help us move the effort along because they realize we are there to help them.

Unfortunately, there seems to be more support out there for dogs caught in ice floes than for dogs trapped by their own unsociable behavior. We'll consider why in the chapters ahead. I'm confident that, together, we can create better possibilities for dogs, especially if we succeed in changing social norms that influence how much we extend ourselves to help dogs with issues.

Social norms are rules that serve as standards of behavior for groups. They "may be internalized, i.e., incorporated within the individual so that there is conformity without external rewards or punishments, or they may be enforced by positive or negative sanctions from without…(and) norms are more specific than values or ideals: (for example) honesty is a general value, but the rules defining what honest behavior in a particular situation is are norms."[1] Over time, social norms can shift and we're the ones to bring about change. If not us, who else?

....
1   *Encyclopedia Britannica*, (n.d) American Psychological Association (APA): social norm. <http://www.dictionary.com/> (accessed May 07, 2009).

Opinion of Experts

> *The world is not run by thought,*
> *nor by imagination, but by opinion.*
> **Elizabeth Drew**

No Shortage of Advice

Before calling in a professional like me, most families have solicited advice from neighbors, friends, relatives, groomers, salespersons in pet stores, animal rescue workers, television shows featuring Hollywood trainers, dog park acquaintances, and others with no training in modern behavioral assessment and techniques, but willing to serve as on-the-spot experts on dog behavior. Trust me: there is no shortage of advice on how to set things straight with the family dog.

Advice can range from, "No wonder you're having problems. You just let your dog walk through the door ahead of you. You have to teach him his place, behind you," to "Use an electronic (shock) collar." If you were sitting where I am you'd have to search hard to find a connection, any connection, between some of the advice delivered with hit-the-nail-on-head certainty and what science tells us are the real-time needs of dogs.

However, there are advantages to collecting advice like this on the fly: it's usually free and, if we don't like it, we can disregard it without feeling like knuckleheads. This might help us understand why so many families make the rounds in their communities, collecting ideas, trying them out, hoping to hit the jackpot with a single intervention that will cancel out the bigger problems.

There is something charming and perhaps ruggedly American about our willingness to ascribe expert status to the many dog lovers in our communities who have a point of view. Of course, we can easily imagine the downside of such an egalitarian approach to problem-solving: that is, the advice dispensed is not apt to fit the dog or situation at hand.

With this in mind, let me ask you: If you had an elementary-aged child who was distressed over separations from you to the point where she refused to go to school, would you take seriously off-the-cuff tips from your child's hairdresser on how to help her? Would you ask her physical education teacher for anything more than a referral to a qualified professional? No, probably you would not. In the United States, we have an abundance of psychotherapists: psychiatrists, psychologists, clinical social workers, applied behavior analysts, and other doctoral and master's level mental health counselors who are considered qualified to do behavior counseling. You would likely turn to them.

In addition, if the teacher told you to use a cattle prod or electronic collar to persuade your child to leave for school in the morning, you might think she'd missed her calling as a comedian. If you discerned she was serious, you might consider the advice, "if you see someone coming to do you a favor, run for your life!"

Returning to psychotherapists, whether they actually help a respectable number of children and families function better is a separate issue but relevant to this discussion about our animal friends. In human mental health, so much depends on the worldview, background, education, and artistry of mental health counselors, and in many cases, the correct application of medications by medical doctors interested in affecting brain functioning in a positive way. In sum, a percentage of psychotherapists are not a "good enough" match for their clients; if not well-matched, more problems may be created than actually resolved through "helping" processes. By "good enough" I mean, facilitates growth, meets needs, and solves problems adequately.

While dogs are inarguably easier to influence than humans, the worldview, background, education and artistry of animal behavior experts and dog's families determine what course will be set for them. In another parallel, veterinarians, as doctors of veterinary medicine, might recommend psychotropic medications for dogs to support well-formed behavior modification and management plans. We should choose any professional with care.

We'll consider the various animal service professions and developing professions in later chapters. I hope to establish that you are apt to lose more than you gain if you expect enthusiastic neighbors, groomers, breeders, veterinarians, and trainers to shed meaningful light on your dog's behavior problems, unless they have the knowledge, training and skills to assess, manage and modify problem behaviors. However, if some of you have access to the information you need from known, reliable sources, you might go it alone and meet with success. It matters that your information comes from reliable sources so there's truth to it and not just idiosyncratically selected belief.

Money Matters

As I write this, consumers are being battered by a recession, a credit crisis, and soaring job losses. They have to pay for essentials such as the mortgage or rent, car payments, insurance, and food. By many reports, families are skipping routine human and animal health care so they can hold onto their homes and pay the outrageously inflated cost of college education for their children. At times like this, families have less discretionary money to pay for animal-related services. It's why I wrote this book for families. Money is clearly a factor when they try to decide between getting professional help for their dogs, asking neighbors for advice, or letting the chips fall where they may.

Many Americans have health insurance for human members of the family that at least partially covers the cost of mental health counseling with different types of providers, and medication evaluations by psychiatrists. The insured usually have to meet co-pays. In contrast, most Americans do not have health insurance for dogs and I don't know of any pet health insurance plan that reimburses for behavior problems. The out-of-pocket cost for most dog behavior consults will generally be much higher than the co-pays for human behavior services.

Even when the economy was strong, behavior services were not high up on the chain of services considered essential for dogs. It was consistent with social norms for families to not expend too many resources on their dogs, even when they thought the economy was booming. If you are reading this book, you are doing something to change the norm.

An Orchestrated Plan

Most of the families who ask me for help with problem dogs have tried a do-it-yourself approach before contacting me. As noted above, families in search of solutions to their dog's behavior problems typically solicit advice from non-experts and follow the same linear pattern: they try one intervention and it fails, so they try another intervention and fail, and they try again and fail again. They go along, experimenting with new interventions until they exhaust the possibilities—and this is central—they exhaust possibilities that may have worked if the stronger interventions had been applied together, as part of an orchestrated plan.

Let me restate this point differently: the ideas families get from other dog enthusiasts are sometimes very good. However, behavior problems typically have diverse causes and are held in place by multiple reinforcers. As such, interventions must be applied in tandem with other promising interventions and not chosen cherry-picker style. I'll illustrate why orchestration matters in case studies throughout the book.

Of course, there are exceptions to every rule. Behavior professionals, me included, do sometimes apply single interventions that end problems with a slam-dunk—and it's most impressive when that happens!—but the larger task is to devise plans that get at the target behaviors from many angles, with an approach that is carefully orchestrated.

> *The best friend a man has in this world may turn against him and become his enemy... The one absolute, unselfish friend that man can have in this selfish world—the one that never deserts him, the one that never proves ungrateful or treacherous—is his dog.*
>
> **George Graham Vest (1830-1904)**

Man's Best Friend

Today's dogs live in-home with us, protect us, brighten our days, and ease our loneliness; they love us with a devotion that touches us, heart and soul. There is extensive research that attests to the health benefits of companion dogs for folks that are beset by health problems.

President Obama and his First Lady Michelle counted on Bo, a Portuguese water dog, to help their children make the adjustment to their new home in the White House. That's a pretty tall order for "just a dog" but who doubts the First Puppy will serve beautifully in his appointed role (especially as he comes to them with training and they've done their homework on puppy care for the breed).

We know these pooches we love are more than "just dogs," don't we?

"Get Rid of the Dog"

In the current economic climate, too many families are telling me they may have to "get rid of" their dogs with annoying or dangerous habits. Isn't it about time we stopped using the pejorative phrase "get rid of" in reference to at-risk dogs? Who has ever "gotten rid of" a loved pet and felt good about it? Our dogs live with us as members of the family. Do we "get rid of" family members when they are going through a rough phase or suffering from some trauma? Let's not "get rid of" any more family dogs.

At this point you might ask, do I think every dog can be saved? No, of course not. There are plenty of dogs that will not hold up in families, no matter what we do. These are the dogs we might let go of, for our safety and well-being and theirs. If we put forth serious effort and engage in a process of deep discernment, we might still have to make the tough choices and then grieve and long for the ones we lost, but we will respect ourselves for having honored the love relationship. What could possibly be better for souls and civilizations than love?

When I was a teenager, I was hired to baby-sit some young children over the summer while their parents worked. The family allowed their little Bichon to run around their large, unfenced property unleashed. One morning, shortly after I arrived, the tiny dog dashed through the trees and into the road and was hit by a car and died. The mother asked me to dispose of the body in the trash, got in her car and raced off to work. I wanted some sort of ceremony (we did have a ceremony) and wondered what it would mean to the children long-term to have their dog "gotten rid of" like that, as if the little fellow that cuddled with them at night didn't matter. As you can imagine, he was more than "just a dog" to them.

A few years later I heard that, tragically, the father and two of the children were hit by a car and killed while trying to cross the same road in the dark. I still worry for the surviving children because the message from their mother about loss of life was that life and love don't matter.

Hold On!

In my role as a dog behavior consultant, I give family members positive messages about the value of life and love as the ultimate expression of our humanity. Love itself is the essential good. We don't say, "It's just love", do we? Nor do we say, "Let's get rid of our love." Standing by our dogs is about respecting ourselves and honoring the love we share with another species and it's about having character and caring for our own.

We need not abandon common sense when we love. We know some dogs will not adapt to anyone's home, whereas others will fail miserably in one home but function well in another, perhaps with a family in a different phase of life or with a lifestyle that's a better match for the dog's temperament and needs.

One impediment to helping our pets, as mentioned, is that most families are challenged by competing needs and diminishing resources. Typically, childless couples can spend more on their dogs and there are obvious reasons for this generosity: in addition to caring, they don't have the other expenses.

Even if we were in a position to spend endlessly on our pets, should we? Any family (with endless resources) has the right to answer the question in ways that are consistent with their own values and priorities. My family doesn't have endless resources so it's a no-brainer: we're do-it-yourselfers and if we have a big problem and can figure out how to fix it ourselves, that's what we will do. We are willing to work to bring about the best outcomes, but in the least expensive ways. This do-it-yourself approach has enabled us to meet our financial obligations and goals, so we're kinda' happy with our choices.

Becoming Experts

As I stated earlier, asking non-experts for advice generally won't get you far. However, dog owners can become knowledgeable enough to handle some problems on their own if the information they acquire is from known, reliable sources. Dogs are simple; it's the misinformation that complicates things. And consider this: to do-it-yourself, you only have to become an expert on the dog you have, not an expert on every dog.

Hopefully, you'll find the views and strategies presented here clear and precise. You'll have to modify them in spots to fit your dogs and to suit your own style and working situations.

Making a Difference

You'll notice I don't draw too many lines in the sand between the owners and professionals who might team up to save a dog, or between the established professions and developing professions. I leave such maneuvering to loyalist members of the various groups. A tremendous manpower shortage exists in the animal behavior professions. There are simply not enough resources anywhere to help all the dogs with behavior issues and it's on this basis that I recognize all available sources of reliable help. Throughout the book I give information and examples to help you differentiate between what's reliable, what likely is not, and when caveat emptor applies. At the top of my reliability hierarchy are the individuals or teams who actually get problems solved and your dog's and family's needs met.

SECTION TWO

ALL
THAT
MATTERS

Theoretical Matters

My approach to animal behavior consulting is rooted in my education and training in psychology and family therapy. Like most counselors, I draw from diverse theoretical models to understand families with dogs and the social systems involved with them. I bring a variety of techniques to the table, ranging from family systems and the structural approach, to interventions from the behavioral and biological modalities. My approach is integrative, or eclectic. I try to do what works and does not cause harm.

While on the surface this section on theory would seem to be of interest only to professionals, there is a plethora of insights to help families understand in-depth how to help dogs, too. So please, read on!

Biological Considerations

A biological approach to behavior modification emphasizes physically determined etiological factors and their manifestations, including psychosomatic effects. It includes the diagnosing by a veterinarian of medical causes for behavior disorders, and the use of psychotropic medications prescribed by veterinarians, when appropriate.

We must always consider that medical problems might be at the root of behavior problems. For example, pain and seizure activity can lead to aggression. In addition, some dogs are genetically wired for aggression, obsessive-compulsive disorders, anxiety or phobias.

Learning Theory & Behavior Modification

Learning theory helps explain how dogs learn in their environments. It amply provides animal behavior professionals with a solid, scientifically supported basis for assessing and modifying problem behaviors. We're doing behavior modification when we apply learning theory to affect change. Any time we modify dog behavior we employ the principles of learning, whether we admit to it or not. If you're new to learning theory, you'll find an excellent introduction to it in Drs. Mary Burch and Jon Bailey's book, *How Dogs Learn.*[7] The concepts that matter most to us relate to the use of positive and negative reinforcers and positive and negative punishers to affect change.

Key Learning Theory Terms Defined

REINFORCERS are used to increase the likelihood that a behavior will be repeated in the future. A POSITIVE REINFORCER is "any event whose presence increases the likelihood that ongoing behavior will recur... A positive reinforcer adds something rewarding to a situation."[8] A NEGATIVE REINFORCER is "any event whose reduction or termination increase the likelihood that ongoing behavior will recur... Negative reinforcement subtracts something unpleasant from a situation."[9]

PUNISHMENTS are applied to decrease the likelihood that unwanted behavior will be repeated in the future. POSITIVE PUNISHMENT involves the presentation of an aversive (unpleasant) stimuli, and negative punishment involves the removal of an appetitive (desirable) stimuli.

The behavior modification approach that educated animal behavior professionals employ is based on empirical methodology. There is a massive (huge!) body of literature attesting to the successful application of behavior modification to train animals and ameliorate a wide variety of problems.

....

7   Mary R. Burch PhD and Jon S. Bailey PhD. *How Dogs Learn* (Howell Book House, 1999).

8   Morris, *Psychology: An Introduction*, 193.

9   Ibid.

The bottom line: with behavior modification we must make it pleasurable for dogs to offer "good" behaviors and we must avoid inadvertently rewarding them for "bad" behaviors. The hitch is we don't control all the reinforcers. "Bad" behaviors, the behavior humans don't want, are quite often "self-reinforcing", meaning they are intrinsically rewarding to dogs. For example, dogs might jump on visitors because it's fun; they steal food from kitchen counters because scavenging is a talent they enjoy and stolen food is yummy.

The challenge for families is to set things up so "good" behaviors are reinforced. This is where empathy helps: if we view the world through our dog's eyes, as our dogs experience life, we can understand what truly satisfies them and what it takes to interest them in offering "good" behaviors, the behaviors we want.

Dogs don't typically differentiate "good" from "bad", or "ethical" from "unethical"; they take their cues from us and go with what feels good. This phenomenon leads to much misunderstanding between the species. Owners can end up in the ridiculous position of trying to convince their dogs they are bad, as in "bad dog!" Owners should ask instead, "What is reinforcing the unwanted behavior?" or "How does the dog benefit from acting that way?" and "How can we change the patterns of reinforcement to get more of the behaviors we want and less of the behaviors we don't want?" It's (sort of) that simple.

Learning theory facilitates objectivity and deters us from anthropomorphizing so much that we can't see our way out of problems. For example, if owners think their dogs have been naughty and must be taught a lesson, what will they do? They will try to force their dogs to behave. The reality is, dogs are not capable of understanding social justice issues in human terms. The challenge for us is to woo them so they want to go our way instead.

When you want to change behavior, start with the following:

- Identify what behaviors you want to reduce.

- Identify what behaviors you want to increase.

- Figure out what reinforces both sets of behaviors.

•   Manipulate the reinforcers to get more of the behaviors you want and less of the behaviors you don't want.

About Reinforcers

Reinforcers either help dogs gain access to pleasant stimuli or escape from unpleasant (aversive) stimuli. A stimulus is "an action, condition, or person that provokes a response, especially a conditioned response".[10] A conditioned response is a response that "becomes associated with a previously unrelated stimulus as a result of pairing the stimulus with another stimulus normally yielding the response".[11] Examples of reinforcers some dogs consider aversive are loud noises, extremes of temperature, unpleasant experiences such as having their nails cut, baths, having to go outside in the rain, being left behind, veterinary visits, and the appearance of people and animals they fear.

The behaviors we want to influence can occur when dogs have been deprived of an essential reinforcer (stimulus)—for example, food, water, exercise, attention, play, petting—and they have to gain access to the reinforcers to meet their needs. Examples of specific reinforcers dogs will work for are treats, belly rubs, chase games, and opportunities to sniff. They will repeat the behaviors they believe brought the good stuff their way. They are less apt to offer behaviors they associate with good stuff that vanishes.

Breed-Specific Reinforcers

When trying to find ways to reward our dogs, to bring about an increase in the behaviors we want and a reduction in the behaviors we don't want, we must consider breed-specific yearnings. Herding dogs such as Border collies and Australian cattle dogs want to chase, bark and nip. Bloodhounds and Beagles are in their element when they are following scents. Hunting and digging are what many terriers, such as Fox terriers, are meant to do; sporting dogs such as German short-haired pointers and Labrador retrievers, may

....

10   *The American Heritage® New Dictionary of Cultural Literacy,* 3rd ed., s.v. stimulus (2005).

11   *Random House Dictionary,* s.v. conditioned response <http://www.dictionary.com> 2009.

love to hunt and retrieve.

All dogs are not born with the innate drives that are typical for their breed. We need look no further than my family's Labrador retriever, Andy, for proof. He has a lovely, mellow temperament but minimal interest in retrieving anything (but food, always food).

Innate behaviors such as herding can be so self-rewarding that even the most dog-friendly rewards, such as the Super-Motivating Treats explained in case studies with a recipe in the "Behavior Cache" section, will fail as reinforcers. A Border collie eying a prospective target might be so hard-wired and enthralled by this activity that he would choose it over high-value treats. A Golden retriever might not be happy on a walk unless he has a stick or leash to carry. The reinforcers you use have to trump naturally occurring reinforcers to get your dog's attention. For example, if you want to interest a stalking Border collie into going with you, you might offer a high-value treat *and* run the other way, so the Border collie has to chase after you to get the treat. As is intuitively obvious, paired reinforcers (more good stuff!) are apt to be more effective than single reinforcers.

More Natural Reinforcers

You can be creative with reinforcers. To be effective, you have to choose reinforcers that are a good fit for the dog you have. It's more efficient to go with the natural flow of your dogs. Rewards can be something as basic as giving your dogs opportunities to explore the outside or perhaps special treats or a ball to chase.

When dogs are tired, sleep is reinforcing. When they are lonely or afraid, the company of trusted companions is most welcome. They tune in to food when they are hungry. There are exceptions of course. We all know of dogs that are like Pippin in the *Lord of the Rings* and want second breakfast morning, noon and night, with equal intensity throughout.

Reinforcers can be anything dogs perceive as rewarding at that moment in time. It can be a challenge to figure out what will work. What is rewarding in the quiet of the home will likely not hold the same appeal when in competition with distractions out on the street.

Approach-Avoidance Conflict: An Example

Fearful dogs confuse us because they might clamor to get in the face of other dogs, when a part of them wishes they could just hide. Like humans, dogs experience approach/avoidance conflicts, or "(conflicts) resulting from the presence of a single goal or desire that is both desirable and undesirable."[12] Dogs that are fearful of other dogs situated at a distance might have excellent interpersonal skills up close, or they may routinely get in to fights when in proximity to other dogs. Either way, if dogs appear to be conflicted and fearful, I encourage families to positively reinforce (reward) them for fleeing the objects of their fear rather than letting the dogs engage and dramatize the events. Dramatizations become habit. When the flight response is solid, typically after some months, the dogs can then be reintroduced quietly to those they once feared. I describe this phenomenon of rewarding dogs for letting go of their interest in "triggers" that typically set them off, in cases throughout the book.

Systems & Structural Change

There is a tendency for living things to join up,
establish linkages, live inside each other,
return to earlier arrangements,
get along whenever possible.
This is the way of the world.

Lewis Thomas, *Lives of a Cell*

With learning theory as one base, you can find other pathways to change if you think about your dogs as systems that benefit and suffer, as we do, through their give and take with other social systems such as extended family, the neighborhood, dog training centers, day-care, kennels, dog parks, veteri-

12 *Mosby's Medical Dictionary,* 8th ed., (Elsevier, 2009).

nary practices, grooming shops and so forth. Each system has a measure of independence from the others, but the systems are interdependent and the influence is reciprocal. That is, intersecting systems both influence and are influenced by other systems, as described below and in the case studies.

If you want to understand systems theory as applied to dogs in families, I recommend you read my 2006 book, *The Family in Dog Behavior Consulting*. The paragraphs that follow are from my text:

"A portion of each dog's behavior is stable. For example, some dogs are more easily aroused and don't react well to novel stimuli. Others are easily aroused and can adjust to the new and unexpected. Some dogs guard precious possessions and others are naturals at offering them up freely, regardless of training. Nevertheless, dogs also evidence behaviors that are rooted in context, with the dog acting and reacting to environmental stimuli."

"Dogs are especially influenced by humans in the families with which they live, and similarly influence their humans' responses to them. For example, a dog with a fearful human handler may develop fears and phobias to rival those of her owner (through owner reinforcement). A hyperactive dog who is punished for misbehavior may become more anxious and destructive as a result. It's clear that dogs can't be fully understood without also considering them within the context of their families. "If I am the singer, you are the song" says the dog with behavior problems."

"For a complete picture, we must consider systemic and environmental influences. A dog's behavior is affected by her relationships with owners, groomers, veterinarians, neighbors, delivery persons, trainers, other animals, and objects in the environment (placement of the crate in relation to humans and placement of the food bowl in relation to other animals' food, etc.) . . . and our behavior is affected by the dog. Thus, the question for us . . . becomes, "What do we need to know about the relationships between dog, family, and environment, to help us formulate accurate and usable assumptions about dogs?" Our next question must be, "What should we then do about it?"[13]

....
13   Lynn Hoover. *The Family in Dog Behavior Consulting* (Dog Quirks LLC, 2006). 8-9.

Veterinary Practice as a Social System

Social systems typically pressure the other systems in their orbit to comply with overt and covert expectations and if the others don't comply they might be made to suffer in some way. For example, your veterinarian is responsible for treating the patients in his care, but he also has the duty to protect employees from bites. If a dog growls at an employee, the veterinarian might write "dangerous dog" on his chart and insist he wear a muzzle for future visits. For your part, you might stay with the practice and let your dog carry the "dangerous" label. You could engage in problem-solving: stay, accustom your dog to the muzzle at home so he's not as stressed over having it on in the veterinary office, and work to modify your dog's fearful response to the veterinarian and staff. Alternatively, you could say "We're outta' here" and switch to a different veterinary practice to give your dog a fresh start. You could then work to ensure your dog has a positive experience with the new practice. As an aside, some families deal successfully with veterinary visits by keeping their dogs in the car until it's time to meet with the veterinarian so they are not stressed by the sights, sounds and activity in waiting rooms. (See "Stress Signs" in the "Behavior Cache" section at the end of the book).

Scrumptious treats, if not prohibited for medical reasons, can take dog's minds off their troubles; massage can help them relax. Some anxious dogs are helped if their families and veterinary staff use happy voices to make the visits sound like more fun than the dogs are anticipating. You can read more about the application of calming strategies in the "Dolly" chapter and in later sections.

If you change practices and your dog doesn't growl at the new veterinarian or staff, you might escape the "dangerous dog" label. The original veterinary practice loses your business but they also gain because they no longer have to deal with a dog that's difficult for them. The new veterinary practice benefits because they get a patient that's easy for them to work with. The larger point here is that a dog that is aggressive in one veterinary office will not necessarily generalize the experience and aggress with a new veterinarian, especially if the family and veterinary staff arrange the setting so the dog has a more positive experience from the outset. New environments are opportunities for dogs to practice more adaptive behaviors.

Strengthening Relationships

Most of us want our problems solved in ways that strengthen relationships with our pets. This can be accomplished by making it enjoyable and in our dog's best interests to do things our way.

It's a surprise to families when they discover how easy it is to lure dogs away from "dark side" behaviors with fun and food and naturally-occurring rewards such as opportunities to sniff. Why use punishment to convince dogs to comply with our wishes when all we have to do is provide reinforcement for good behavior? Positive reinforcement is less risky than punishment and it stands to reason that it does more to enhance relationships. The families I work with feel better about themselves, even triumphant, when they apply rewards-based strategies to get the behavior they want from their dogs. Humans know they have achieved something special when they successfully solve problems in a compassionate way.

Changing the Structure of Systems

We can alter behavior, emotional experience, and relationships by changing the position of people and animals in systems and by interrupting the usual patterns. If I looked at client families solely through the lens of learning theory I would not see these possibilities.

For example, a couple called me to help with a very shy, sensitive Spaniel they rescued from a shelter. The Spaniel presented as attached to the husband and shrinking with fear from the wife, who wondered what she had done to make him dislike her. The harder she tried, the worse the dog seemed to feel about her. He had a history of nipping at visitors who got too close and she feared he would bite her. Significantly, the wife was convinced she was not good for him. On this basis, she wanted the dog gone.

I understood that what she really wanted was to be free of her guilt. As surely as Shakespeare's Lady Macbeth sought to rid herself of guilt over her part in the killing of Duncan when she uttered those infamous words "out damn'd spot", the wife's mantra may as well have been "out damn'd dog". The difference is, my client was clearly not guilty. She just felt guilty.

The guilt impediment originated with a dog trainer the couple hired to come to their home before they found me. The trainer blamed the wife: "He wasn't like this when you brought him home. What did you do to him?" Knowing as I did that the wife's guilt distracted her from problem-solving, I sought to detoxify the situation in this way:

I asked the wife to cook a hot dog on the stove while the husband and I stood at a distance (I know, hot dogs aren't health foods, but they sure are good…). Not surprisingly, the dog gravitated to the wife and her hot dogs. Per my instructions, the wife put hot dog bits on a plate and brought them with her to a chair, where she sat down. When I tried to approach the dog he growled at me, as he typically does in response to approaches by the wife and other "strangers". The husband was sitting in another chair, but where do you think the dog went for protection from me? He went to the Hot Dog Lady! He leaned against her, almost hugging her with his body, with one eye on the hot dogs and the other, a fearful eye, fixed on me. She became his new "Best Friend" and I became the "Scary One", from the fickle Spaniel's perspective.

The Spaniel's pattern was to align himself with a "Special Someone" and look to that person for protection from the Scary Ones. The good news is, at least he was not afraid of everyone! I used myself in a purposeful way to change the structure of the system and show the wife that the dog's selection of friends and his imaginings about Scary Ones was not personal. It was not about her. It was just something he did in relationships while concurrently endearing himself to the Special Someone's in his life.

After this, with her guilt vanquished, the wife didn't want to send the dog back to the shelter. This was a good thing for Mr. Dog—he would have been euthanized because he now had a bite history. The couple succeeded in modifying some of the fear-based escalation to aggression though the relationship never became good enough. The couple ended up rehoming him with a single woman, a dog groomer who doesn't get much company so he doesn't have opportunities to rebound off of Scary Ones. He has his Special Someone and she adores him. I consider this a positive outcome: we kept things going and succeeded at getting the dog to a safe harbor where his emotional and structural needs were immediately met better than in his previous home.

At this point you might ask, why didn't I just tell the wife the other trainer was wrong and the dog's spookiness with her was not her fault? First, though she liked and trusted me, she wouldn't have believed me in a visceral way; she needed a real-time encounter with the truth. I have confidence in families: if the answers were easy to assimilate they would have figured things out for themselves. Second, she did indeed have a role in the dog's dysfunction, as do most owners. She's one of those lovely people who, when they encounter problems, have to get in there and fix things. She kept trying to fix things for the dog and her pestering caused him to become even more apprehensive about her.

In family systems terms we call this phenomenon "complementarity"—two or three members get caught up in a reciprocal pattern that inhibits problem-solving. It's not the owner's fault and it's not the dog's fault; it's just something that transpires when they are together. My purpose was to help them arrive at a more functional "complementarity".

You'll come across examples throughout the book of the application of systems theory to animal behavior consulting. If you want to understand the structural perspective in greater depth, I recommend you read Dr. Minuchin's book, *Family Healing: Strategies for Hope and Understanding*.[14] It's a fun read and the case studies are fascinating. Dr. Minuchin, a psychiatrist and founder of structural family therapy, is renowned as a gifted storyteller and healer of families.)

In sum, general systems theory applied in tandem with learning theory confers on us a powerhouse of options for helping families with dogs. The real gift of systems theory is the assurance that everyone matters, in a non-hierarchical way. This perspective shows us how to bring about the best of possible outcome for everyone in the system.

14   Dr. S. Minuchin and M. Nichols M.D.. *Family Healing: Strategies for Hope and Understanding* (Free Press, 1998).

Relationship Matters

Dogs Vote for Positive Reinforcement

When we ask dogs what training methods they like best, they tell us through their behavior that they, of course, prefer rewards over punishment. Dogs similarly tell us what goodies, toys and attention make the best reinforcers. They enjoy figuring out how to get good stuff from us. There's a positive training "movement" afoot in this country and it's considered "dog-friendly". We can empathize with dogs in this regard: who among us would not want to be positively reinforced for offering behaviors that are pleasing to others?

Positive Methods are Effective

Today's behavior professionals trust rewards-based methods because, when properly applied, they are highly effective. Why risk the negative side effects that can accrue if we use punishment? In addition, choosing the least intrusive and minimally aversive methods (LIMA) available is obviously ethical, especially when they work as well or better than punishment-based approaches.

Dogs respond with exquisite sensitivity to simple cues. In spite of this, many dog owners believe they have a mandate to teach dogs that they, not the dogs, are the ones in charge. Humans are the leaders, dogs are supposed to follow along. Leadership surely matters in our relationships with dogs, but the surpassing challenge is to help dogs understand what we want from them, and to teach them acceptable behaviors to replace the unacceptable ones that bring them into conflict with us. Asserting our leadership over dogs doesn't call for a big splash. In truth, it's surprisingly easy to take the lead. Simply ask a dog to sit, and when he sits he has deferred to your leadership. Without any drama, the dog affirms that you are solidly in charge. That is what it takes to establish leadership with dogs.

A Little Punishment Goes a Long Way

Some trainers argue that punishment has no place in training and they'll not admit that a well-timed correction has surely saved the day for some dogs. My clients point this out to me often. For example, one man whose dog bit him told me, "Uncle Harry used to bop his dog on the chin and he never tried to bite him again!" This may or may not be true: as we reviewed Uncle Harry's life we discovered the dog was later euthanized for unspecified reasons. Be that as it may, the most reliable and ethical plans to manage and modify dog behavior have rewards-based methods at their core.

A study published in the *Applied Animal Behavior Science* journal showed that "25 percent of dogs trained with "aversive" techniques reacted to their training with an aggressive response of their own. Dogs trained in a more positive, encouraging manner, by contrast, showed almost no aggressive behavior."[15] On the flip side, 75 percent of dogs trained with aversives apparently did not become aggressive. It's an issue that should be approached in a nuanced way.

We Understand Positive Reinforcement

Most of us are not strangers to positive reinforcement. Indeed, rewards-based methods form the foundation for educating our children. "Spare the rod, spoil the child" has been in the dust bin, where it belongs, for several generations. Nevertheless, a percentage of families still believe they have to be macho for their dogs or their dogs won't respect them. But dogs are like us: they respond well to firm but loving guidance. Why would we conspire to instill fear in them when they naturally want to live peacefully with us?

....

15   Sophia Yin, DVM, MS. "New Study Finds Popular Alpha Dog Training Techniques Can Cause More Harm Than Good". <http://www.askdryin.com> March 9, 2009.

Dog-Friendly Training

I use the term "dog-friendly" with some reluctance because trainers who apply punishments more freely have been characterized, in contrast, as not friendly to dogs. This can be a projection; sometimes the inverse is true. I've worked with dogs that experience some of the so-called "dog-friendly" methods and tools as aversive because they were misapplied. For example, a clicker is rightly considered to be "dog-friendly" though it can be highly stressful to dogs to have the clicker used excessively and with poor timing. Nevertheless, my stance on punishment coincided with that of the American Veterinary Society of Animal Behavior (AVSAB), long before they issued the statement below:

The Use of Punishment for Behavior Modification in Animals

"AVSAB recommends that training should focus on reinforcing desired behaviors, removing the reinforcer for inappropriate behaviors, and addressing the emotional state and environmental conditions driving the undesirable behavior. This approach promotes a better understanding of the pet's behavior and better awareness of how humans may have inadvertently contributed to the development of the undesirable behavior. Punishment should only be used when the above approach has failed despite an adequate effort as part of a larger training or behavior modification program that incorporates reinforcement of appropriate behaviors and works to change the underlying cause of the problem behavior."[16]

People-Friendly?

I'm concerned when animal service providers aren't charitable in their views of colleagues or clients who make choices counter to their own beliefs, values and ethics. The high-road response is to try to understand perspectives that are different from our own. It's troubling to me when we make assumptions about the "opposition" that may not be true. This requires the use of a

----

16   AVSAB Position Statement, "The Use of Punishment for Behavior Modification in Animals". American Veterinary Society of Animal Behavior <http://www.avsabonline.org>.

defense mechanism called projection. Projection is "the tendency to ascribe to another person feelings, thoughts, or attitudes present in oneself, or to regard external reality as embodying such feelings, thoughts, etc., in some way."[17] This can result in defamation, "the act of defaming; false or unjustified injury of the good reputation of another, as by slander or libel."[18] Individuals who are people-friendly promote positive regard, tolerance, and acceptance of differences. I think we can agree that dogs and humans would be better served if harsh judgment of humans was not intermingled with dog-friendly agendas.

We make nuisances of ourselves when we try to advance our agendas dogmatically (no pun intended), especially if we convey that we are "better than" those who don't hold our beliefs. It's usually not possible to get others to learn and problem-solve with us if they feel we are looking down on them. I hope you will join me in advocating for people-friendly cultures where other points of view are respected and differences can be negotiated.

Training Tools

One big issue in dispute is the use of choke chains, prong, or electronic collars. Most groups of "dog-friendly" trainers oppose the use of these tools. This is not the problem, as I see it: we are all called to take a stand on the issues of our day (in a people-friendly way). As Martin Luther King said, "Our lives begin to end the day we become silent about things that matter." However, we err when we take our arguments to the extreme, as in "No, never!" and make pejorative comments about those who use such tools. We especially fail as human beings if we engage in negative campaigning against people who admit there is a place, even if it is a small one, for these collars in their training toolboxes.

Other examples of aversives, or punishers, are shake cans (put pennies in a can and shake it), spraying dog's faces with water, leash pops, alpha rolls

---

17   *Random House Dictionary*, s.v. projection <http://www.dictionary.com>.
18   Ibid s.v. defamation .

(rolling dogs upside down to establish dominance). I would agree that these types of interventions are usually unnecessary. We have modern techniques and tools that are effective and less risky. Alpha rolls are a bit dramatic when all we have to do to establish leadership is ask our dogs to sit.

The issue of tools is certainly important and arguments against the use of some old-fashioned tools have merit. Indeed, the AVSAB issued the following statement on tools:

> "Punishment: (i.e. choke chains, pinch collars, and electronic collars) should not be used as a first-line or early-use treatment for behavior problems. This is due to the potential adverse effects which include but are not limited to: inhibition of learning, increased fear-related and aggressive behaviors, and injury to animals and people interacting with animals."[19]

In our role as behavior service providers, we undoubtedly do have to make recommendations about tools and training methods to accomplish mutual goals. However, we're being paid to do this as professional problem-solvers, not as proselytizers trying to win converts.

Positive Regard

Animal behavior professionals must have the knowledge, skill and professional formation to negotiate differences without stressing systems, and that starts with positive regard and the realization that we have an ethical obligation to try to respect those differences.

Role of Education

Harvard University, in a report on the purpose of education, wrote, "The aim of a liberal education is to unsettle presumptions, to de-familiarize the familiar, to reveal what is going on beneath and behind appearances, to disorient young people and to help them to find ways to reorient themselves."[20]

....

19   AVSAB Position Statement, "The Use of Punishment for Behavior Modification in Animals", <http://www.avsabonline.org>.

20   Task Force on General Education (TFGE). General Education Gains . *Harvard Magazine*. (January 2, 2007). <http://www.fas.harvard.edu/~secfas/Gen_Ed_Prelim_Report.htm>.

In it's booklet, *Essays on General Education*, Harvard University posits that general education "teaches students to understand themselves as products of—and participants in—traditions of art, ideas, and values. General education develops student's understanding of the ethical dimension of what we do."[21]

We might suppose that education would help us make our way through discussions without maligning others in a personal way. Perhaps the behavior professionals who come to our homes should have to meet minimal education requirements before hanging out their shingles?

At this point some readers will want to make the point, "we know of educated professionals who can't handle differences and they routinely characterize the opposition in pejorative terms." Of course, this is true. During our worst moments we might even be describing ourselves. However, education, especially in the helping professions, supports the development of positive regard, professionalism and ethics in receptive students.

Extreme vs. Moderate Views

Extremism can be understood as "a tendency or disposition to go to extremes or an instance of going to extremes, especially in political matters."[22] Extreme in this context means exceeding the bounds of moderation. Extremism tends to take the form of "no never… yes always… always bad… always equally bad."

As for activism on behalf of animals, the use of "direct, often confrontational action… in opposition to or support of a cause"[23], has undoubtedly resulted in improved conditions for some animals. There is certainly a place for activism in the world of dogs, and perhaps it should have an honored place. However, activist groups tend to espouse more extreme views. Extremism in a *consulting situation* is problematic if it clouds judgment and interferes with the professional's ability to assess situations objectively. For example, a behavior professional with extreme views might see a client with an aggressive dog using one of the tools they are against, such as an electronic containment

---

21   Ibid.

22   *Random House Dictionary*, s.v. extremism <http://www.dictionary.com>.

23   *The American Heritage® Dictionary of the English Language*, 4th ed., s.v. activism (2005).

system or prong collar, and conclude without reflection that the use of the tool caused the dog to become aggressive. This may or may not be true. What is true is that professionals should withhold judgment until all the information is in, and they must consider a wide range of possible explanations for a dog's behavior. When we are responsible for assessing clinical situations, we especially must differentiate between established fact and personal bias.

A moderate is "a person who is moderate in opinion or opposed to extreme views and actions."[24] We might suppose, as evidenced by the definitions alone, that extremists are on a collision course with moderates. Moderates might leave room on the spectrum for extremists, but extremists are not inclined to make way for moderation. If a moderate questions the "no, never" beliefs of extremists, some extremist will paint the moderate as "the Other", a supporter of whatever it is they are against. If a moderate says, for example, "I can think of an occasional valid use for an electronic collar; years ago I had a case…", the extremist might chastise the moderate publicly and accuse the moderate of being an advocate for shock collars, and at his worst, try to turn others against the moderate. I've seen this happen, though not all extremists operate with apparent narcissism.

Another type of problem occurs when those espousing extreme views make it hard for moderates to usher in middle-ground change. Extremists say "no never!" Moderates say "maybe sometimes" and especially, "We're here for a purpose. Let's get the problem solved."

In sum, extremist trendsetters might win converts, but they turn a lot of people off to the very change they are trying to effect. Moderates don't get in the way of change, but they may have more trouble getting heard over the roar and threat of extremists.

Wisdom

Dr. George Valliant, a psychiatrist and Harvard professor, spent over thirty years as Director of the Study of Adult Development. This study charted the

---

24   *Random House Dictionary*, s.v. moderate <http://www.dictionary.com>.

lives of 824 men and women for over 60 years. He is the author of numerous books including *Adaptation to Life*, and the insightful *Spiritual Evolution: A Scientific Defense of Faith*. He wrote that wisdom is "an awareness that all judgments are a function of, and are relative to, a given culture and personal value system."[25]

Few would claim all educated individuals are wise, or people-friendly for that matter, but higher education is meant to help the receptive acquire wisdom; at its best it provides platforms of support for positive regard.

Empathy, Projection and Differences

> *If hominids called hobbits, extinct little people, are a separate species, it is a reminder that life is a problem for which the solutions are many.* [26]

About empathy, projection and selfishness Valliant said: "Brutality occurs when projection replaces empathy…Selfishness is not susceptible to another's point of view…(and) the (real) danger is the lack of empathy…"[27] Empathy might be the first casualty of vigilantism that often accompanies extremism. I hope you will agree, movements that don't rely on projection and defamation to accomplish worthwhile goals are more worthy of our respect.

As adults, we constantly interact with people whose point of view is different from our own. The challenge for humans is to respect others in spite of differences. We might do well if we aspire to the Golden Rule to "do to others as we would have them do to us".

For example, before attaching labels to others such as, "You're unethical" because they engage in behavior that violates our principles, we must consider the possibility that the Other might be highly ethical, but adhere to principles

---

25   George Vaillant, M.D.. *Spiritual Evolution: A Scientific Defense of Faith* (Broadway Books, 2008).

26   Editorial, "Hobbits and Hominids" Editorial. *New York Times* (May 2, 2009).

27   Valliant *Spiritual Evolution*, 79.

and values different from our own.

Alternatively, the Others might simply have fears that are different from our fears. Most of us can't handle every situation we encounter with the same high level of integrity and competence. Occasionally we find ourselves in over our heads. Life has its disappointments and sometimes we even have reason to be disappointed with ourselves.

Here's an example of a respectful response contrasted with an unfriendly one:

A person who has figured out how to disagree respectfully and means well might say, "I hear what you're saying. I agree with you on point one, that's a good one, but I don't agree on point two and here's why..."

A person who is projecting might respond with: "You're so wrong. I've always wondered about your ethics", or "You're pathetic", or the decidedly unfriendly, "I feel sorry for you", and then make pejorative comments about the opposition behind their back. This occurs partially when people who are projecting don't have the ability to stay with issues that are up for discussion.

Empathy vs. Projection

Going through my cases, I see that a high percentage of my clients report they were subject to verbal abuse by service providers over issues relating to their dogs. A common scenario occurs when clients call breeders to report their puppies are reactive and showing signs of aggression and what should they do about it? One typical non-useful response from breeders is to project blame on to the family, "It's your fault, what did you do to that puppy?" instead of engaging in a discussion to try to determine in a nuanced way the likely contributing factors and possible solutions.

Some breeders may react defensively because they don't want it known that puppies from their litters have problems with aggression or anxiety, or perhaps they lack the skills to help buyers deal with behavior problems. To really understand anyone's motivation, we have to ask them and make it safe for them to speak their truth.

In another scenario, a Toy dog growled at the veterinarian's staff and my client admitted the dog also growled at visitors and neighbors at home. When the technician asked, presumptively, when my client wanted to have the dog spayed, my client responded truthfully that she did not want her beautiful, little, albeit cranky dog, spayed, because she planned to breed her. The technician proceeded to berate her for wanting to breed a dog that was known to be aggressive. The technician called my client "irresponsible" and stated angrily, it was "unbelievable!" that she would want to breed this dog.

To clarify, the thinking among many dog professionals, me included, is that aggression can have a genetic base and if "it's in the genes", aggressive dogs should be altered so they can't have puppies that might also become aggressive. (There's research to support the link between genes and behavior in humans and animals.) My client, in her defense, did not have a clue about genes, aggression and brain disorders (or breeding), and she rightly knew of no concrete evidence to support the technician's claim that her dog's aggression had a genetic base

The veterinarian in this scenario, caught in the middle, jumped to the technician's, not my client's defense. Their collective response left my client feeling embarrassed, upset and abandoned. On the spot, she decided to switch veterinary practices and asked the new practice for a referral to me for help with the aggression. Interestingly, in the new veterinary office, the staff was empathic towards the little dog and my client, and the dog didn't growl at anyone there. This gave the dog a much-needed fresh start with veterinarians.

At this point you might think, "But the veterinary staff is right! She shouldn't breed that dog!" This might be true, but with the information you have, how can you be sure? As it happens, this dog had minimal early socialization, which might partially account for her fear-based aggression. We were quickly able to modify the aggression. Whatever the truth, it doesn't help when we verbally assault clients, colleagues, or anyone, especially as a first-line attempt to influence their behavior. If we are to believe Valliant, empathy is good, whereas projection is not.

Self-Awareness & Empathy

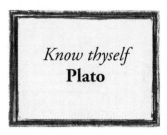

Know thyself
Plato

Educators in the helping professions take seriously the maxim "know thyself". Counselors in training are expected to become aware of their values, beliefs, preferences, the organizing principles of their lives, and the ongoing interplay between themselves and their families. Knowing who we are helps us view others with clarity. Some of us learn tolerance from our families-of-origin and life experiences, others learn more through formal education.

Self-awareness gives us the ability to connect empathically with our own and other species. If we know who we are, we can view the world through other's eyes, see what they see, feel what they are feeling, and assess what they value and need most, without losing touch with what we see, feel, value and need. In sum, we can enter into another's worldview without losing sight of our own.

Sympathy & Empathy

Sympathy is not the same as empathy. As I wrote in my *Family in Dog Behavior Consulting* text, "The most important insight I can give you about empathy is that it is not the same as sympathy. The sympathetic person feels sorry for people. He recognizes they are at a disadvantage and feels compassion and pity for their misfortune and distress."[28] Sympathy doesn't feel as good to the receiver as empathy. The sympathetic might pity us but stay at arm's length from our suffering. We could be in a room filled with people who sympathize with us and feel quite alone.

Conversely, the empathetic are there with us, as companions for the journey.

28 Lynn Hoover, *The Family in Dog Behavior Consulting*, 130.

Empathy does not look down but reaches across and takes us in. Empathetic persons identify with us and understand our situation, feelings and motives. They share our experiences, feel our pain, and because of them we are less alone in the world.

Differentiation of Self

Psychiatrist Dr. Murray Bowen developed the "differentiation of self" concept to help us understand emotional maturity and our striving for self-definition from a family systems perspective. The concept "describes the fact that people are not the same in terms of the way they manage individuality and togetherness in their lives. People can be viewed as existing on a continuum, a continuum called the scale of differentiation, ranging from the lowest to the highest levels of differentiation of self."[29] Less differentiated people are more often awash in a sea of emotionality, and more easily swayed by emotionality in groups. Bowen would have us aspire to higher levels of differentiation of self.

As we evolve, we learn to articulate, "This is who I am, this is what I believe, and these are the lines over which I will not cross." To the degree that solid self exists within the individual, "it permits him to not be totally at the mercy of emotional pressures from groups to think and act in certain ways. It is that part of the individual's functioning that is not dependent on relationship forces to support it."[30] People who reach higher levels of differentiation of self can make their own decisions independent of others around them, and independent of groups, and feel good about themselves and their choices.

Self-Determination

Self-determination is about respecting another's right to decide in accordance with their own values and principles, irrespective of the values we hold dear. For example, we must neither condemn nor rhapsodize about families who love their dogs so much they will tolerate bites to their children (though we must protect the children!). Similarly, we neither castigate nor applaud

....
29 Michael Kerr, M.D., "Family Systems Theory and Therapy" in *Handbook of Family Therapy*, eds. A. Gurman and D. Kniskern. (New York: Brunner/Mazel, 1981) 247.
30 Ibid.

families who opt for euthanasia the first time the dog bites a child (though we must protect the dog!). We are charged with introducing information to expand their worldview and giving them opportunities to think about issues in ways not previously considered.

Standards for Animal Behavior Professionals

Self-determination, a nonjudgmental approach and positive regard are the core values of helping professions; there's a body of research that supports the selection of these values as worth embracing. Behavior professionals who go to client's homes must be held to high standards of professionalism because they gather private information from families before it's been established they can be trusted to process the information in a reliable way. Families especially need behavior professionals who will not enter their homes and judge what they see. Fidelity to the core values goes hand-in-hand with the helping profession's duty to protect the public from abuse, including harsh judgment.

Call to Action

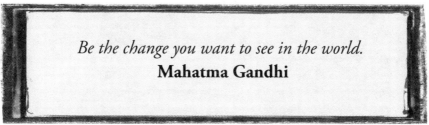

Be the change you want to see in the world.
Mahatma Gandhi

In sum, empathy, compassion, and positive regard are high-road responses. Most would agree that projection, selfishness, and disrespect are low road. At this point, I hope I can count on you to call dog service providers, especially behavior professionals, to task for low-road responses. Our support for the animal behavior community must go to those who are willing to take a stand to combat cultures that promote projection and shoot the legs out from under those with empathy for humans and animals. However, let us go gently, for "in a gentle way you can shake the world."[31]

----

31 Mahatma Gandhi. No source listed.

Professional Matters

The best dog behavior professionals are the ones that help get our problems solved. They can assess situations accurately and connect us with the appropriate interventions. They show us how to get into good-enough relationships with our dogs. The challenge is to identify a single such expert in our community. We don't usually have the option of interviewing several candidates to find one who is compatible plus, has the knowledge, skill, imagination, and ethics to create a viable plan and interact with us productively.

The animal behavior fields are for the most part unregulated. Anyone can claim expertise. Anyone can call himself a "behaviorist" and charge money for his services. Anyone can imagine he knows more than he does.

In contrast, when we search for human health care providers in our communities, whether it is medical doctors or nutritionists, psychiatrists or mental health counselors, we choose from among licensed and certified professionals we know have met minimal standards for their professions. We still must exercise good judgment but at least it's evident who is in the ballpark of qualified practitioners. Among animal behavior service providers, anyone can put himself in the ballpark.

Search for Animal Behavior Professional

We have two applied animal behavior professions (veterinary behaviorists, applied animal behaviorists) that have "legitimacy", meaning they are formed in accordance with established principles and standards for the education and credentialing of members. The numbers in each group are quite small. Most would agree the shortage of qualified candidates works to the detriment of animals.

"A profession is a vocation founded upon specialized educational training, the purpose of which is to supply disinterested counsel and service to others, for a direct and definite compensation, wholly apart from expectation of other business gain".[32] Note that professionalism calls for *disinterested* counsel and service. Let's add that to our emerging definition of people-friendly. Synonyms for disinterested (as an adjective) are "impartial, neutral, unprejudiced, dispassionate". Antonyms are "partial" and "biased."[33] Note: I'm aware of more refined definitions of a "profession" that I don't address here.

VETERINARY BEHAVIORISTS

Is there a Veterinary Behaviorist Near You?

- Search the list of board certified veterinary behaviorists at www.dacvb.org.

Veterinary behaviorists are licensed veterinarians and board certified by the American College of Veterinary Behaviorists. They completed an undergraduate college degree, veterinary medical school and a residency with extensive education in veterinary behavior. They have "conducted original research, published findings in academic journals, and passed a rigorous exam. The veterinary behaviorist can fully evaluate the pet, both medically and behaviorally, and is trained to recognize where an underlying medical condition may either cause or contribute to a behavior problem. Once a behavior problem is diagnosed, a behavior modification plan will be explained and/ or demonstrated to the owner. In addition, the veterinary behaviorist can use their combined understanding of pet health and behavior to determine when and if a psychotropic drug may be a useful adjunct in the treatment of a pet's behavior problem."[34]

....

32 Architects Services , *New Statesman,* (21 April 1917). (Article by the Webbs quoted with approval in paragraph 123 of a report by the UK Competition Commission, 8 November 1977).

33 *Random House Dictionary,* s.v. disinterested <http://www.dictionary.com>.

34 American College of Veterinary Behaviorists, <http://www.dacvb.org>.

The problem with veterinary behaviorists is there are so few of them. At the time of this writing, there are less than 50, not all in practice, and some work in clusters so many states don't have a single veterinary behaviorist within their borders. Even if there is one in your community, she may not be a good match for your family or your dog.

To put the shortage problem in perspective, in human health care there are over 45,000 medical doctor psychiatrists in the United States plus hundreds of thousands of non-physician mental health care providers delivering the bulk of psychotherapy, including behavior modification and management. We have lots to choose from in our communities and if we disagree with the recommendations of one professional we can move on to another. This is the healthier scenario.

Veterinary behaviorists are less apt to do home visits though some ask families to bring along video footage of events in the home. They may not have the same technical skills as dog trainers who devote all of their years to teaching dogs new behaviors. Veterinary behaviorists are held to refined codes of ethics and understand professionalism and their responsibility to serve dispassionately, without significant bias about client concerns. As a group, they have taken positions that emanate, I believe, from a deep sense of ethics and commitment to the well-being of animals.

CERTIFIED APPLIED ANIMAL BEHAVIORISTS (CAAB)

Certified Applied Animal Behaviorist Qualifications

- Obtained an undergraduate degree at an accredited college or university.

- Gained admission to an accredited graduate school or veterinary school through a highly competitive admission process.

- Completed post-graduate education receiving a Master's or PhD degree in a behavioral science, or DVM (doctor of veterinary medicine) or VMD (veterinary medical doctor) degree with a behavioral residency.

- Completed a post-graduate education receiving a Master's or PhD degree in a behavioral science.

- Passed rigorous oral and written examinations given by their faculty committees.

- Published articles in scientific journals.

- Supervised hands-on experience with animals.

- Met the course work and experience requirements for certification as set forth by the Animal Behavior Society.[35]

CAAB's graduate degrees are in related scientific fields such as psychology, ethology, biology, and zoology. "Their education...qualifies them to evaluate a pet's behavior problems, determine why it is behaving inappropriately, and tailor a behavior modification program for the individual pet...they should work closely with the veterinarian in the follow-up care of the pet's behavior problem."[36]

As non-veterinarians, applied animal behaviorists don't prescribe medications or diagnose medical problems. At this time, there are less than 30 CAAB's in 18 states and not all of them are in practice. Many do make home visits or ask for video footage. They are bound to an evolved code of ethics and aspire to professionalism. Their approach to the truth, like that of veterinary behaviorists and other scientists, is not likely to be casual. Some of the more illuminating and scientifically valid textbooks and articles on dog behavior were written by CAAB's. Their contributions are significant.

A potential downside: while applied animal behaviorists were in college learning about topics far removed from daily living with companion animals, some dog trainers were full-time hands-on with dogs. Most applied animal behaviorists will not have completed a single course (for credit from a recognized accredited institution) specific to dog behavior problems, though there is no reason to believe they have not self-educated to state-of-the-art levels. In addition, some applied animal behaviorists have not completed course-

....

35   The Animal Behavior Society, <http://www.AnimalBehavior.org>
36   The Animal Behavior Society is the organization that certifies Applied Animal Behaviorists.

work in clinical interviewing or other aspects relating to the human dimension though many undoubtedly self-educate successfully in these areas, too.

Applied animal behaviorists don't have to pass a qualifying examination for certification; as such, their species-specific learning (dogs living in relationship with humans) may not have been subjected to objective measure, though their overall learning and capabilities have been measured exhaustively through traditional academic channels using many different types of measures, objective and subjective, over a number of years.

I make these points because a key issue between the well-formed and the developing professions is, do some practitioners have the capacity to self-educate to state-of-the-art levels in areas where there are gaps in their education? I believe there is sufficient evidence to demonstrate that some do.

Is there a Certified Applied Animal Behaviorist Near You?

- Search at www.certifiedanimalbehaviorist.com

Related Professions

VETERINARIANS WITH INTEREST AND EXPERIENCE IN BEHAVIOR

From the American Veterinary Society of Animal Behavior's Web site: "There are many veterinarians in general practice who are not board certified specialists but have considerable interest and experience in the field of behavior. These individuals, though licensed veterinarians, may not have completed the training necessary to become specialists. Due to their high level of interest, they have often attended extra hours of continuing education programs and may be very familiar with the latest research and knowledge in the field of behavior. Veterinarians with this level of interest and dedication to the field may be very well qualified, experienced, and committed to helping pet owners understand and correct behavior problems in their pets."[37]

Is there a Veterinarian with an Interest in Dog Behavior Problems Near You?

Search at the Web site of the American Veterinary Society of Animal Behavior (AVSAB), www.avsabonline.org.

Veterinarians with an interest in behavior generally have not had their dog behavioral knowledge and skills assessed using reliable measures, though as the AVSAB statement acknowledges, some veterinarians do acquire the requisite knowledge and skills beyond veterinary school through *self-education* and continuing education. A distinct advantage to going with a veterinarian is they can prescribe medications and diagnose medical problems. A disadvantage might surface if they prescribe medications in situations where a nonmedical service provider might know how to get by without medicating.

CERTIFIED/LICENSED MENTAL HEALTH PROFESSIONALS, APPLIED BEHAVIOR ANALYSTS, AND TEACHERS AS DOG BEHAVIOR CONSULTANTS

A larger number of human mental health professionals, applied behavior analysts, and teachers offer dog behavior consulting services. These professionals gained admission, through competitive processes, to accredited colleges and universities. They earned undergraduate degrees and completed their studies at the master's (MA/MS/MSW/MFT, MEd) and/or doctoral level (PhD), in regulated fields such as mental health counseling, psychology, family therapy, clinical social work, applied behavior analysis, teaching, etc. Most participated in clinical practicums and had to pass licensing and/or certification exams in their respective fields. Their knowledge and competency were measured in many way. They are held to refined codes of ethics by their professional associations. They usually have interviewing skills and may have more than a casual approach to the truth with a respect for research. On the downside, their learning about dog behavior problems most often has not been measured, though their judgment and ability to assess and plan effectively will

37   American Veterinary Society of Animal Behavior (AVSAB), <http://www.avsabonline.org>.

usually have been assessed using a variety of measures over time. Some in this group are also accomplished dog trainers and have passed objective qualifying examinations on training (through the Certification Council for Professional Dog Trainers, for example), though they would not have been measured for their knowledge of dog behavior problems.

My Background. I'll use myself as an example because I'm in this group. I earned an undergraduate (BA) degree in psychology and clinical social work, a master's in social work (MSW) with a clinical concentration, and I completed a year-long post-master's program in marriage and family therapy. I passed qualifying exams for certification and licensing in clinical social work, and marriage and family therapy, and overcame many hurdles to earn and maintain eligibility for Clinical membership in the American Association for Marriage and Family Therapy (AAMFT). I completed mandatory continuing education requirements over many years to retain licenses and certifications. I care passionately about the truth and refer often to research.

I have a love for animals and a talent for forming relationships with them. While raising our children, I trained service dogs for clients with disabilities. As I became aware of gaps in service for dogs with behavior problems, it was a natural progression to an applied dog behavior field. I did endless reading and worked hands-on with dogs to learn all I could about dog behavior. I have an extensive library of books, videos and articles written by well-known, reliable sources, and I attend and present at seminars and conferences. There was a huge learning curve. I've been in practice as a dog behavior consultant for more than ten years now and it's been a very enjoyable adventure. It's reasonably easy to get most dogs to change their behavior and my people skills serve me well. Of greatest import, I know how to assess and tie assessments to meaningful interventions, because my education and experience prepared me for this.

Need for Representation and Measures of Learning. A number of my colleagues are like me and responsibly self-educated in areas where they had deficits. It's likely they have the knowledge, skills, and ethics to work effectively, and objectively, on behalf of dogs and families. This group of professionals, with master's and/or doctoral degrees in related fields, needs professional representation by an association with solid requirements. Most of all, there's a need for objective measures to assess their learning about dogs and dog behavior problems. This group brings so many strengths to the table that I see them as potentially being on par with the applied animal behaviorists.

The key point some of my colleagues seem to be missing is that humans, as bipedal primates, belong to the Homo sapien species. In other words, humans are animals too. If we have the capacity to work with human behavior problems, and are naturals with animals, we can learn to assess and manage dog behavior problems. The limitation is, we haven't had our learning measured.

Who Qualifies? Non-veterinarians don't diagnose medical disorders, recommend medical treatments or prescribe medications. Some (veterinarians) believe only veterinarians should be allowed to provide animal behavior services on the basis that most problems have an organic base; others believe the few applied animal behaviorists should be included but with no other avenues for entry to the field.

However, in human mental health, the bulk of psychotherapy and counseling services are provided by psychologists and other mental health counselors with master's degrees from recognized accredited schools, for problems with an organic base. They are not medical doctors. I don't see why the standards would be different, or "higher", for animals, especially when it's clear many non-veterinarians have learned how to competently manage and modify dog behavior. Indeed, some of the highest-contributing books were written by non-veterinarians and non-behaviorists who by most accounts, are practicing at state-of-the-art levels. In addition, it's simply ludicrous to maintain that less than a hundred individuals in the whole world should be the ones permitted to help companion animals with issues when the need is so great (as in millions) and the evidence not only suggests but otherwise proves that self-educated human mental health professionals, applied behavior analysts, and some teachers and trainers do help.

If we are committed to reducing the number of dogs being inappropriately punished, discarded, or euthanized for behavior problems that are resolvable, and to increasing the number of dogs and families who are satisfied with their relationships, we must figure out how to make good use of all existing human resources. On the other hand, searching outside the established professions has its clear and seemingly insurmountable drawbacks and gives weight to the concerns of nay-sayers. I address the prime issues below.

The Developing Professions

Dog Behavior Consultants And Counselors

I've long been an advocate for professionalizing the field of dog behavior consulting or counseling, and dog training. As such, I founded the International Association of Animal Behavior Consultants[38], in 2003 and served as president, and chair of the Dog division, for four years, though I later rescinded my membership over the issue of certification.

Several other organizations are evolving. For example, the Association of Companion Animal Behavior Counselors[39], lists practitioners with an interest in behavior; some have completed course work in an affiliated training program with many measures of learning, and some have graduate degrees in mental health or related fields.

Problems with Resistance. There is a resistance to professionalizing the fields of dog behavior consulting and dog training with the resistance coming predominantly from those who don't have degrees in related fields. The understandable concern is the unnecessary hurdles that might prevent qualified, capable people from contributing to the well-being of animals with issues. We all know of behavior consultants and trainers who are doing high-caliber work and some have little or no college education. A few have published books and articles; some contain reliable and scientifically valid information.

Duty to Protect. Professional membership associations must promote the interests of members but their overriding responsibility is to protect the public. The big question is, does the work of behavior consulting require learning a specialized body of pedagogical knowledge and a specialized set of skills? Most of us would agree it certainly does. Reliable assessment and effective intervention depends on a specific knowledge base and requires intensive study and training, with standards to ensure only qualified candidates enter the field.

....

38   International Association of Animal Behavior Consultants, Inc., <http://www.iaabc.org>.
39   Association of Companion Animal Behavior Counselors, <http://www.animalbehaviorcounselors.org>.

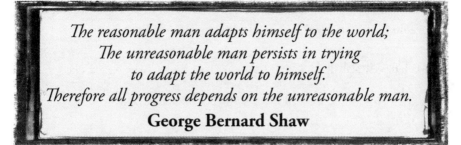

The reasonable man adapts himself to the world;
The unreasonable man persists in trying
to adapt the world to himself.
Therefore all progress depends on the unreasonable man.
George Bernard Shaw

Reliable Measures of Learning. The recognized accredited colleges and universities must have a significant role. The fact of practitioner shortages must not result in a diminution of standards, though we must show creativity in our search for solutions. We hopefully will not leave high-functioning practitioners behind because they lack academic credentials. However, there is a need for reliable, valid, and varied types of measures so candidate's learning and skill development can be assessed in many ways over time. Some measurements must be taken by independent bodies whose responsibilities are to assess learning. Without reliable measures, candidates are passed by guesswork; credentialing can be politicized with the unqualified passed along with the qualified. Some may be rejected because of where they stand positionally in their groups. This is not acceptable. The educational system in our country is designed to circumvent these all too human problems that occur in groups that take on evaluative functions and credentialing.

Dog Trainers

The Greek philosopher Aristotle wrote: "People become builders by building and instrumentalists by playing instruments." We might presume people become dog trainers by training dogs. Many devote their adult years to learning everything they can about dogs. It's impressive to see so many of them care.

The Association of Pet Dog Trainers (APDT)[40], founded by veterinarian Dr. Ian Dunbar, spawned the Certification Council for Professional Dog Trainers (CCPDT)[41] an independent entity that tests trainers for their knowledge of

....
40   Association of Pet Dog Trainers, <http://www.apdt.org>.
41   Certification Council for Professional Dog Trainers, <http://www.ccpdt.org>.

learning theory and the application of behavior modification, canine ethology, animal husbandry, teaching techniques, classroom management, and more. The exam is not qualifying for behavior, or diagnostic, interviewing and relationship skills, and it's oriented to trainers who teach classes. The CCPDT may eventually have an exam to test behavior knowledge and skills.

The APDT favors "dog-friendly" methods but its mission is to educate so it remains inclusive; the APDT does not exclude trainers who use different methodologies. As such, it does not screen out applicants for membership on the basis of methods used.

The International Association of Canine Professionals[42] (IACP) represents dog trainers and other canine professionals such as dog walkers, groomers, kennel owners, pet sitters and retailers. The IACP supports a broad range of methods and has traditionally been more accepting of the use of positive punishment in training, sometimes over positive reinforcement. I suspect if the dog-friendly folks were more people-friendly there would be more integration and modernization of methods within the groups.

Interplay of Non-Medical Behavior Service Providers with Veterinarians

Veterinarians today have to work with different species of animals and must be current in many areas: cardiology, neurology, orthopedics, oral surgery, rheumatology, orthopedic surgery, geriatrics, and so on. With all of this on their plates, it's unrealistic and I believe inhumane to expect veterinarians to also be current on the nuances of behavioral care. As such, I provide scientifically sound information on medications and behavior-associated medical conditions to veterinarians, to improve the chances of successful outcomes with their patients. I can do this because of my strong background in health care, dog behavior problems, and information research. Animal behavior professionals can learn how to handle information exchanges with respect to copyrights and other legalities from the Association of Independent Information Professionals[43] (AIIP). Dog's families can do their own information

---

42   International Association of Canine Professionals, <http://canineprofessionals.com>.

43   Association of Independent Information Professionals, <http://www.aiip.org>.

searches if they can handle the terminology and discern between reliable and unreliable sources of information

When we consider what is wrong with America's dogs, problems occur because usable, scientifically valid behavior information is not getting to the families who would benefit most from it. A lot of junk information is getting through, however. As such, I searched for a model that would get scientifically valid behavior information to veterinarians and other dog service providers and dogs' families, while respecting professional boundaries. I looked to the Association of Independent Information Professionals and the Collaborative Family Healthcare Coalition[44] (CFHA) for working models.

I collect information about dog behavior issues put forth by known, reliable sources such as veterinary behaviorists, applied animal behaviorists, and ethologists, and pass the information along to veterinarians, or if necessary, directly to families and rescue organizations. I drafted and refined the statement below on Collaborative Care. It details the role non-veterinarians can play in getting information to those likely to benefit most from it.

Collaborative Consulting Model

The Collaborative Consulting Model calls for seamless cooperation and an exchange of usable information between the animal behavior professional, client, veterinarian, and/or veterinary behaviorist. Others, including but not limited to groomers, breeders, extended family, and trainers, may also be included, depending on the issues. Animal behavior professionals optimize opportunities to help dogs by establishing relationships with client families and by facilitating referrals to and from veterinarians. Animal behavior professionals do what they can to ensure clients are informed and veterinarians have the information they need to make the optimal decisions. This might mean the animal behavior consultant sends the client to a veterinarian or veterinary behaviorist with a written report, establishes contact by phone, or does information research and provides usable information in the form of articles containing

---

44 Collaborative Family Healthcare Coalition, <http://www.cfha.net>.

scientifically valid information.

Non-medical animal behavior professionals are aware of laws in their states governing the practice of veterinary medicine. They are not to practice veterinary medicine without a license. As such, non-medical animal behavior professionals do not advise on medical issues, drugs or diet. However, they may research and make information from known reliable sources available to veterinarians, colleagues and clients. Reliable sources would include leading members of the veterinary and applied animal behavior communities and peer-reviewed journals.

In Sum

You might find practitioners with an interest and expertise in behavior in your community, outside of the more developed professions (veterinary behaviorists, certified applied animal behaviorists) though you must assess individual qualifications independently and with caveat emptor, let the buyer beware.

A good starting point for most families is to get a referral from a trusted veterinarian who is privy to feedback from client families who have used the behavior professional's services and are reliable reporters. Most of my referrals come from veterinarians.

Another strategy with obvious limitations is to find behaviorists in your yellow pages phone book (usually under "Dog Trainers" or "Pet Trainers") or on the membership association's sites. I encourage you to peruse Web sites and e-mail or call prospective behavior professionals with questions about their education, training philosophy, and background. Some professionals will not accept clients if there seems to be a high degree of mistrust at the outset so handle your inquiries respectfully.

I hope this book helps you find behavior professionals or trainers in your community that can meet your dog's needs and treat your family to positive regard and confidentiality. Alternatively, you should be able to solve some problems on your own.

SECTION THREE

CASE STUDIES

Dolly's Enthusiasms

Dolly Madison is named after one of the best known and best loved First Ladies to have ever inhabited the White House. Margaret Bayard Smith, a chronicler of early life in Washington, D.C., wrote appreciatively about President Madison's wife: "It would be absolutely impossible for any one to behave with more perfect propriety than she did."[45] Dolly the dog is similarly well known in her community and much loved. We are confident she will live up to her namesake in good manners, some day. Even the First Lady had to pass through adolescence to reach propriety.[46]

Dolly's Problem

"I'M SO EXCITED, I JUST CAN'T HIDE IT"

All the neighbors (except for one) make a fuss over Dolly Madison when she blows through. Dolly, in turn, makes quite a fuss over her neighbors. She made quite a fuss over me when we first met, nipping at my shirt and pants and zipping around behind me to climb on my back when all I asked for was a friendly paw shake. She is just as apt to climb all over her family when they try to pet her and on her worst naughty-dog days she tears at their clothes and jumps at them without restraint. Some neighbors and relatives mistake her enthusiasms for friendliness. Her people knew there was something more going on inside and that's why they asked their veterinarian for a referral.

....

45 Margaret Bayard Smith, *The First Forty Years of Washington Society in the Family Letters of Margaret Bayard Smith,* ed. Gaillard Hunt (New York: Frederick Ungar Publishing, 1965). 62.

46 *Random House Dictionary,* s.v. propriety <http://www.dictionary.com> (accessed May 12, 2009).

Complex Explanation

DEVELOPMENTAL STAGE: ADOLESCENCE

Our explanations, or constructions, about why dogs behave as they do drive us to decide what we will do to counteract unwanted behavior and improve a dog's quality of life. At the time of the consult, Dolly was fourteen months old. Adolescence lasts from about four and a half months to two or two and a half years. I wrote earlier about the hidden value of anthropomorphisms. To understand adolescence in dogs, here is the place where we can anthropomorphize without restraint and not distort meaning. Think about the teenagers you have known: high-spirited, pushing the limits, rebellious, inattentive, uncertain, in-your-face, but lovable nonetheless. In both species, human and dog, the teenage brains are not as developed as the bodies.

EVOLUTION OF HABITS

Dolly is a teenager and this partially explains why she exhibits such rude (as it seems to us) greeting behavior. One difference between the species is that with teenagers we can usually wait things out, with confidence they will outgrow their immaturities, return to earlier, family-instilled values, and discover themselves in the process. With dogs, however, if we let adolescent high jinks become habit, the misbehavior is apt to continue unabated for the rest of their lives. This is a key point about dogs: if "bad" behaviors are repeated they quickly become habit. Our task is to ensure that "good" behaviors, the behaviors we want, get repeated and become habit instead.

"Bad" behavior can also intensify with age. For example, as dogs transition from adolescence to adulthood, they might become bolder and more willing to use aggressive strategies to conquer their fears; other dogs become cranky and lose their inhibitions as they move through old age.

A WELL-TRAINED DOG?

It might be tempting to view Dolly as unschooled. "She needs obedience training!" However, Dolly is a reasonably well-trained dog. She breezed through puppy kindergarten and Canine Good Citizen (CGC) classes, passing eight out of ten CGC tests of required skills. The American Kennel Club's (AKC's)

Canine Good Citizen Program (CGC) "stresses responsible dog ownership for owners and basic training and good manners for dogs" and "is designed to recognize dogs who have good manners at home and in the community."[47]

Dolly failed to earn her CGC award because, as might be expected, she couldn't sit still for petting and she failed the test that calls for a supervised separation. As instructed, Mary, her person, left her with an evaluator, walked off, and tried to stay out of sight for three minutes. The test is meant to "demonstrate that a dog can be left with a trusted person, if necessary, and will maintain training and good manners."[48] When it was Dolly's turn to be "abandoned", she became frantic, and I understand she turned some pretty amazing somersaults to get to Mary. Obedience training had not changed how she felt about being left behind.

SEPARATION DISTRESS?

From the information we have, we might wonder if Dolly is at-risk for separation anxiety, a problem that is difficult to address because it occurs when humans are not there to help their dogs. However, when Dolly's family goes away, she handles being home alone without apparent incident. I say "apparent" because, how do we know what dogs do when we're not with them, unless we leave a video camera on or the dogs do damage to the house that is evident on our return? Most dogs with significant problems dealing with separations do leave observable damage to their homes or self from their desperate attempts to reunite with their owners. Dolly left no such evidence.

We might surmise from her behavior that Dolly's stressed and feels anxious when she's separated from Mary in a public setting, and she feels safer and better protected when she's with Mary. Most dogs that are bonded in a healthy way to their humans appear to feel safer when they are with them. A small percentage of dogs suffer horribly when they are left behind.

The information about Dolly's handling of separation suggests she is more anxious and reactive in settings where other people and dogs are present than in the safety of her home when nothing stimulating is going on. If Dolly's

---

47   AKC Web site, CGC program, <http://www.akc.org/>.
48   <http://www.akc.org/events/cgc/index.cfm>.

family had not provided her with a quiet home where she feels safe, it is likely she would not handle their leaving her home alone as well as she does.

SUBSTITUTE SPECIAL PERSON

During the test, Dolly may have known her special person was out of sight but still there. How would she have responded if Mary left the premises altogether and stayed away for a day? After some time, if the stranger was kind to her and assumed an appropriate leadership role, Dolly might have started to relate to the stranger as a friend, another special person with whom she could feel safe.

The CGC test for supervised separations was given in the same place where Dolly had gone for training since she was ten weeks old. With her sensitive temperament, the classes might have been stressful for her and she relied extra on her special person to face the challenges of that environment. To test this hypothesis, we could take Dolly to a place where she's usually relaxed and having fun, hand her over to a responsible person, on-leash, and ask her special person to leave the room. If Dolly didn't react negatively to the separation, we might conclude the setting of the training center was a source of anxiety for her. We didn't test this because we didn't have to understand this dynamic to modify her greeting behavior. Mary was usually with her, didn't leave her with strangers, and didn't intend to take her back to the old training site for any reason.

BREED-SPECIFIC TENDENCIES

Dolly is of mixed descent—parts Pomeranian, Beagle and Spaniel. I don't know what to make of this breed mix other than to tell you she's beautiful at thirty pounds, with Spaniel-like wisps of hair, and has a "soft" temperament that requires sensitive handling.

EARLY HISTORY

Her family adopted her from a shelter at the age of eight weeks, widely considered the optimal age for puppies to be separated from their mothers and litter mates. We don't have information about what went on during her first eight weeks or information about her mother, father or siblings. It's possible a parent and some, possibly all, siblings struggle with shyness, have problems with impulse control, and rev up as Dolly does.

Another possibility is that Dolly was removed from her litter prematurely and this caused her to develop atypical attachment behaviors. Fortunately, we can help Dolly without knowing for sure if premature separation contributed to adjustment problems.

The most likely explanation for Dolly's behavior is that her pattern of escalation is related to activity in her brain that has a genetic base. Her problems are undoubtedly owner and trainer-shaped but they are not owner or trainer-created.

SOCIALIZATION

Dolly's family knew to socialize their puppy to humans and dogs in many shapes and sizes—people in hats and wheelchairs, babies, toddlers, groups of children and teenagers, older people with canes, disabled people with atypical movements, loud people with big movements, big dogs and little dogs, etc.—before the critical age of twelve weeks. An important caveat to the advice to socialize, socialize, socialize by twelve weeks is the experiences must be reasonably enjoyable; families must be ready to protect their puppies if they are feeling more than a little stressed or afraid. (See "Stress" in the "Behavior Cache" section.)

SOCIALIZATION AND VACCINATION DEBATE

Families should also check with their veterinarians to determine what's safe to do with puppies before they receive all of their vaccinations. Keeping them holed up at home is not an option for owners who want a behaviorally healthy dog. They must be socialized by twelve weeks, with a few caveats. For example, it would not be wise to take a young puppy to a dog park for socialization. There may be dogs that are not current on their shots, have transmittable diseases, or behavioral issues such as aggression towards puppies. Families have to balance between competing interests and find ways to protect their puppy's experience and yet provide opportunities for much-needed socialization. Puppy owners are faced with a "you're not allowed to do this but you must do it anyway" dilemma that is not easily resolved. Some families invite other puppies that are similarly in the midst of getting their shots to their homes for play dates and hope for the best.

FIRING UP

Some dogs go from relaxed to over-the-top in an instant. Woomf! Dolly, for her part, revs up slowly. Her greetings are initially appropriate and irresistibly sweet, and that is why she is the darling of the neighborhood. But she soon escalates to super-excited, with jumping and biting at hands and sleeves and ripping clothes; she keeps going with no discernable off-switch. This behavior started when she was a puppy, at around twelve weeks, though she was "always very active and always mouthing and biting."

It is interesting to note that when Dolly's owners return home she waits quietly for them to open the door to her crate. "Sometimes she'll sit there for minutes before she wanders out." This reported information is consistent with the pattern described of slow arousal.

Dolly's greetings became more intense with adolescence. Now fourteen months old, her family reports no recent changes in severity or frequency. She reacts the same to people and dogs and is the same with males and females. There is not anyone she doesn't do this with. She often "appears frightened initially" before the clawing and pawing begins. Mary reports she's worse when she's tired. She sometimes urinates on the spot when she's meeting and greeting.

In my interactions with Dolly, she relaxed when I spoke in a soothing voice and calmed down when I made myself small. She appeared afraid and shrank away when my movements were big or my voice forceful. When I moved to interrupt the greeting behavior she showed mildly fearful behavior, shrinking away from me.

THE FAMILY SYSTEM

Dolly's family consists of two friends, Mary and Janet, sharing a house during their retirement years. They impressed me as quiet by nature, energetic enough for Dolly, and steady, reliable problem-solvers. Experienced dog owners, they didn't have these problems with past dogs. When Mary's late, much-loved, rescued dog died, Mary adopted Dolly from a shelter for altruistic reasons. She had no hidden agendas for Dolly—she just wanted to love and care for her with the same devotion she has shown all the dogs that she has had in her care. Janet was supportive of Mary's handling of Dolly.

Asked what they liked about Dolly, Mary said, "Dolly's a great companion and most of the time a gentle, pleasant dog. She loves to play and walk. She's very loving. We'd like to let her interact more with the neighbors when we walk but can't because of her jumping."

By their report, there have been no changes in the household to explain Dolly's problems. She's always been like this. She's not a problem in any other way. Dolly doesn't growl when petted and has no issues with grooming or other handling efforts. Mary and Janet can, for example, lift her up and move her off of furniture. She occasionally growls, as dogs do, when she's playing or chewing on a toy. She's fully housetrained.

ROLE OF THE DOG TRAINER

When Mary asked the trainer who led Dolly's Puppy Kindergarten and Canine Good Citizen (CGC) classes what she should do about Dolly's behavior problems, the instructor said, "just keep working with her." Mary was skeptical about the trainer's advice. She understood that more training was not the answer and hoped for a game plan that described specifically what they should do to manage and modify Dolly's behavior. I was delighted by her request because I knew I could deliver an effective plan and was confident Dolly and her family would have happier lives as a result of our work together.

The trainer taught positive methods and Mary had not used punishment to counter Dolly's greeting behavior. If punishment had been used, Dolly may have been more fearful and could have resorted to aggression to chase away the objects of her fears instead of climbing all over them in a somewhat friendly way that may have bolstered her sagging confidence.

IN-HOME ENVIRONMENT

Dolly's being raised in a home without children, with people who are quiet and peaceful by nature. It is hard to imagine a better home for her than the one she is in.

Dolly's people provide her with toys and opportunities that stave off boredom. She is not left alone for more than a few hours at a time.

IN THE 'HOOD

Dolly's neighborhood is busy with people and dogs moving around. The humans approach Dolly in a friendly way, stooping down to pet her and talking to her with soft voices. There is one neighbor who is a little afraid of dogs and she ignores Dolly completely.

Here is a key piece of information that illustrates how details matter: Dolly is at her best during encounters with the neighbor who avoids her! She lies down, waits patiently and doesn't try to interact with her.

Dolly hasn't had much opportunity to be around children with their high-pitched voices and quick movements but when she is with them she's not aggressive or especially fearful though she does get super-excited in the pattern described above.

She is friendly with dogs though she bites at them and climbs all over them, Dolly-style. When she was one year old she had to interact with a relative's two large Labrador retrievers and was "very frightened".

DIET AND HEALTH ISSUES

Dolly eats one of the higher-rated natural foods. (See "Finding Top Foods" in the "Behavior Cache" section.) She is free-fed meaning the kibble is left out all day in a bowl and she can eat from it when she wants. Mary describes her as a finicky eater, and "If she hasn't eaten enough the night before she throws up in the morning." Mary reports Dolly isn't very interested in food and isn't food-motivated.

HAND-FEEDING

During Puppy Kindergarten, the dog trainer asked the participants to hand-feed their puppies all of their meals. Dolly wasn't allowed to eat unless she performed on command for Mary, who followed the trainer's advice pretty religiously: Dolly had to work for her food.

Hand-feeding can be used successfully with some dogs to enhance obedience and bonding with owners. I've recommended some of my client families go to hand-feeding to counteract long-standing training problems. However, Dolly was not a good match for this practice. It's likely hand-feeding was stressful for her. She may have developed an aversion to food partially because the rigors of hand-feeding caused her to feel anxious when she ate.

When assessing dogs, we must consider a full range of possible explanations for their behavior. It's also possible that Dolly has an undiagnosed, and at this time possibly un-diagnosable, digestive disorder. Her veterinarian was tracking her digestive problems.

CARSICKNESS

Dolly gets Dramamine for car sickness and her family tried some Bach herbal remedies recommended by a pet store owner, to calm her. One of the herbal calming mixes made her lethargic, barely able to stand. After this, Mary was reluctant to administer any remedies that had not been recommended by her veterinarian.

SLEEP

Dolly's crate-trained and sleeps in her kennel at night. She also stays in the kennel when her family goes out, never for longer than a few hours. Mary put up an exercise pen (x-pen) in the family room where they gather so Dolly could be with her people and visitors, and yet she couldn't bite them because she was contained. (You can find x-pens in all sizes; they can be used for indoor or outdoor confinement.)

When puppies are crate-raised, as Dolly was, they are apt to welcome the comfort of downtime in their crates. Dolly's people wisely put soft bedding and chew toys in with her. Puppies left without age-appropriate chew toys are apt to chew their bedding.

EXERCISE, PLAY AND TOYS

Flexi-Leash. Dolly gets exercise with three or four walks a day of one half to one mile each. She actually travels further because Mary uses a flexi-leash with a 60-foot circumference. Some trainers are opposed to the flexis because owners don't have as much control and there's the danger the dog might dart into traffic. However, flexis give dogs freedoms and exercise. Most dogs like to sniff and run from place to place and they are not apt to get their fill from walks with traditional leashes and humans setting the pace. The other point is that dogs are not well-served if we put up more red lights than green lights, more no-can-do's than can-do.

Dolly loves her squeaky chew toys and enjoys games of chase and tug.

When Dolly was in classes, her trainer recommended a front-clip harness for all the dogs and that is what Mary used for walks instead of a collar or regular harness.[49] I also recommend front-clip harnesses for some dogs; they work wonders on many dedicated pullers. However, Dolly's a jumper, not a puller, and the harness was unnecessarily restricting her movements and reducing her comfort on walks. (Go to the manufacturer's Web site for instructions on the fit and use of their harnesses.)

In the best of circumstances, the front-clip harness instantly brings a halt to pulling. I worked with a five-year-old boy who was on the autistic spectrum and his service dog in training, a bouncy adolescent (8 month old) Golden Retriever. We fitted the dog with a front-clip harness and took her to a mall. The Golden didn't pull once. The five-year-old was a competent dog handler and the harness inhibited her pulling. Families that have tried choke and prong collars and head halters, unsuccessfully, are surprised at what these simple harnesses can do. However amazing they may be, a front-clip harness was not a good match for Dolly. As partial explanation, Dolly had to wear one prematurely, before she was pulling on-leash.

Interventions:
Behavior Modification & Management Planning

ACHIEVING EQUANIMITY, THE QUALITY OF CALM

Most dogs benefit from relaxation strategies tailored to them. The key to introducing relaxers is to first introduce them when dogs are in a situation where they are already relaxed and nothing else is going on. Our goal is to get the dogs in our care used to achieving maximum relaxation with soothing

---

49   SENSE-ation harnesses, <http://www.softouchconcepts.com/> and Locatis Front Clip harnesses, < http://locatis.typepad.com/home/2005/11/front_clip_harn.html >.

music, massage, acupressure, stroking, TTouch, anxiety wraps, dog appeasing pheromones, medication, and so on. Once dogs are accustomed to relaxing, the relaxation tools can be used in higher stress situations. If we wait until dogs are in high-stress situations and then introduce the relaxers, dogs might learn the wrong lesson: to tune them out and forge ahead in dramatic ways.

USE OF SOUND

Voice. As you may recall, when I spoke in a low, soothing voice, Dolly calmed down. When I raised my voice, she revved up. Her responses told me we could use soft sound to soothe her. This is a convenient tool because it is built in and we can easily change our voice tone.

Music. Sue Raimond is a pioneer of harp therapy for dogs and is also an expert in the field of cytocymaics and vibroacoustics pertaining to the harp. I recommend her CD *Wait for the Sunset*, billed as "the #1 CD for animals!"[50] (For additional sources of music that is soothing to dogs see "Music for Calm" in the "Behavior Cache" section.)

TOUCH

Research shows that long strokes are more soothing than just petting. Mary agreed to use long strokes to help Dolly relax, as long as Dolly didn't bite her moving hand.

Dog massage or TTouch videos[51] can assist, or families might learn canine acupressure to relax muscle tension and relieve stress. Mary quickly picked up the few massage strokes I showed her. She could then quietly reach over and soothe Dolly to help her remain calm during greetings. The real plus with massage is our abilities to deliver are built-in.

DOG APPEASING PHEROMONES (DAP)

A few of my client families report success using DAP devices to help their dogs relax. I know of no good peer reviewed studies that show DAPs are effective. A recent literature review by Dr. Diane Frank, a veterinary behavior-

....

50   Sue Raimond, <http://www.petpause2000.com>.

51   Tellington Touch, or TTouch for Dogs, <http://www.training-dogs.com/tellington-touch.html>.

ist, calls the effectiveness of these products into question.[52]

ANXIETY WRAPS

Anxious dogs might not care much for hugging though some respond well to swaddling, which involves the use of binding to wrap them tightly. You can buy an Anxiety Wrap on the Internet in your dog's size.[53] They're designed to rely on maintained pressure to reduce fear and anxiety in dogs. A similar effect can be achieved using ace bandages, polo pony leg wraps or T-shirts. Mary figured out an adorable, original solution. She measured Dolly's circumference and found a colorful toddler-sized T-shirt wrap with Velcro at a local Walmart for a couple of dollars. Mary put it on Dolly during a quiet time at home and she immediately zonked out. Dolly's pictured above in her wrap.

DR. KAREN OVERALL'S RELAXATION PROTOCOL

Veterinary behaviorist Dr. Karen Overall's "Protocol for Relaxation" is avail-

....

52   Diane Frank, DVM, DACVB, B. Beauchamp, PhD, C. Palestrini, DVM, PhD. "Systematic review of the use of pheromones for treatment of undesirable behavior in cats and dogs. J. of American Veterinary Medical Association. June 15, 2010, Vol. 236, No. 12, p. 1308-1316.
53   The Anxiety Wrap, <http://www.anxietywrap.com/>.

able on the Internet[54], as is her "Treating Anxiety is Different than 'Managing' the Problem", another article I sometimes recommend for families with anxious dogs.[55] They offer strategies for helping dogs relax. I didn't recommend these for Dolly at the outset because obedience training in the past seems to have exacerbated her problems and I wanted to avoid using interventions that required she do anything or have to exhibit self-control on command. I didn't want Dolly to have to act better at this point; I wanted her to feel better and the better behavior would follow.

LIMITING VISUAL FIELDS

With dogs that react to visuals, we can get them through some situations by limiting what they can see so they remain below threshold, which gives them opportunities to learn new behaviors. A threshold is "the point at which a stimulus is of sufficient intensity to begin to produce an effect."[56]

To limit Dolly's visual field, I suggested Mary attach a flag or cloth to a dowel stick (purchased at a sewing store). As soon as she spotted a visual that typically triggers an overreaction from Dolly, Mary would unfurl the flag so Dolly couldn't see the stimuli.

CALMING CAP

A Gentle Leader Calming Cap is another option for limiting visual fields.[57] It might be effective in the car, for veterinary office visits, and nail trimming. It's not a likely option for neighborhood walks, for the obvious reason that dogs must see where they are going. Calming Caps cover the head and must be introduced slowly so dogs are given time to get used to wearing them in advance of an event. Before making a purchase like this, you should see what happens when you gently cover your dog's eyes. If having the eyes covered does not help him settle down, a calming cap might not be the right tool for your dog.

LIMITING SOUND

These days you can actually buy earmuffs for dogs. Check out Mutt Muffs,

54   Karen Overall, <http://www.dogscouts.org/Protocol_for_relaxation.html/>.

55   *DVM Veterinary Newsmagazine*, <http://www.veterinarynews.dvm360.com>.

56   *Random House Dictionary*, s.v. threshold <http://www.dictionary.com>.

57   Gentle Leader Calming Cap, <http://www.amazon.com>, and <http://www.premier.com>.

"the world's only over-the-head hearing protector for animals....designed not to block out all sound, but to be a passive, noise reducing device that will make...time spent in any noisy environment...a comfortable experience for your dog".[58] The trick of course is to match them with a dog that won't take them off. The other catch is, dogs can't put on their own muffs and their people have to be there to supervise. I do have one client who used Mutt Muffs successfully on their storm phobic Golden Retriever.

MEDICATIONS

Psychotropic medications can help dogs get through frightening experiences like thunderstorms. An excellent, informative article by veterinary behaviorist Dr. Karen Overall, "Storm Phobias" is available on the Internet.[59]

A SYSTEMS INTERVENTION: NEIGHBORS AS ALLIES

From Dolly's perspective, the neighbor who ignores her is the best neighbor a dog with her issues could have. When Mary talks to this neighbor, instead of pouncing all over her, Dolly naps. When Mary realized how good this was for Dolly, she asked all the neighbors to stop giving Dolly attention. No petting, no baby talk, they were asked to act as if she wasn't even there. The neighbors were not too happy about this but eventually complied.

OPTING OUT

Conventional wisdom would have us teaching Dolly to sit quietly for petting and greetings. We'd expect her to show good manners in situations that typically trigger reactivity. However, doing the obvious has not helped Dolly in the past. More pointedly, Dolly tells us through her behavior that she can't handle greetings, so why would we have her greet people at all? Why not teach her to avoid the point of "collision" instead?

Arousal and agitation are automatic responses stemming from activity in a dog's brain and nervous system. "The nervous system is a network of specialized cells that communicate information about an organism's surroundings

....

58   Mutt Muffs, <http://earplug-store.stores.yahoo.com/mumufordo.html>.

59   Karen L. Overall, VMD, PhD, Dipl. ACVB. "Storm Phobias", *DVM Newsmagazine*, Sept 1, 2004. <http://www.veterinarynews.dvm360.com/>.

and itself. It processes this information and causes reactions in other parts of the body."[60]

Dogs can't control their own physiological processes and obedience training doesn't change genetic makeup. A viable alternative that creates a win-win for all parties is to teach reactive dogs to let go of their interest in triggers and divert their attention to pleasing positive reinforcers instead. I call this learned tune-out protocol "Opting Out".

I was confident we could teach Dolly to routinely let go of her interest in people and dogs in situations that triggered her reactivity. She'd be satisfied because of the delicious and fun rewards she would get when she went with our diversions. As such, when we saw Dolly start to become aroused, we squeaked toys (with a pronounced squeak) to get her immediate attention. We then lured her with food and other reinforcers to get her to move with us, away from her triggers. We might take her away at a 45-degree angle or turn around completely and lure her in an opposite direction.

The intervention is not as simple as I describe.

The "Opting Out" protocol is about conditioning dogs to experience powerful, positive emotions when they know a named, high-value reward is available. We introduce the Super-Motivating treats to get automatic responses from our dogs. Dogs' interest in the super-motivating reinforcers is meant to trump other interests dogs have. For most dogs, Chicken Meatballs make the perfect Super-Motivating treat. (The recipe and instructions for using are in the "Behavior Cache" section under "Super-Motivating Treats". Check with your veterinarian if you have questions about ingredients.)

The challenge families face relates to timing. We have to distract our dogs and lure them away from their triggers, when they are just revving up and before they become fully reactive. This is because, once dogs are fully reactive to the triggers, they're gone, outside of our sphere of influence. It's too late to modify target behaviors. At that point, when we fail to intervene early enough, the most we can accomplish is damage control that occurs when we physically remove dogs from a scene that typically triggers reactivity.

....

60   *Wikipedia,* s.v. nervous system , <http://www.en.wikipedia.org/wiki/Nervous_system>.

It's easy to catch Dolly below threshold because, as noted earlier, she's unusually slow to rev up. I didn't have to worry about Mary's timing.

We also err when we intervene too early, before dogs notice the trigger. No harm is done, however; the dogs enjoy the rewards we give them though they don't learn anything about handling their encounters with triggers. If we intervene too late, on the other hand, dogs practice their "bad" habits, and the behaviors we want to change become more entrenched.

We tried to figure out at what distance Dolly could be from triggers before she reacted. An occasional dogs will react to a trigger that's moving from a football field away. Dolly reacted within thirty feet.

You might ask, does this mean Dolly will have to live out her years without much contact with people? As you'll see, six months later, when Dolly was free of the habit of climbing all over people, she could be eased into greeting people again.

Behavior planning is about respecting the dogs we have, not the dogs we wish for, not the Hollywood dogs we encounter on television, and not the dog next door who never seems to do anything wrong. The reality is many dogs are easily over stimulated by interactions with others, and we can help them.

TRAINING TOOLS

Dolly didn't need the front-clip harness; it interrupted her free movement and enjoyment on walks. Mary switched her to a regular harness instead and continued using the flexi-leash so she could sniff and run around. What's significant is, she didn't tune in to triggers when she was sniffing and running. Many reactive dogs do, and these dogs need more structured walks, with their attention drawn to their person, who mentally engages them in various activities that serve as distractions from triggers.

Walking. Walks on leashes at a pace set and enforced by humans doesn't do much for a lot of dogs. Just watch what dogs do when they're outdoors and free to run around. They follow scents, stop often, trot over to new spots, touch base with their people, and wander off again. If we want to use walks for positive reinforcement, we must let dogs move about in their own way, unless there's a compelling reason not to let them have these freedoms on-leash.

Mary continued using the flexi-leash because she could handle it safely and Dolly got more exercise this way, and more room to run freely.

Food as a Reinforcer. When I met Dolly she was stressed by food rewards. They were more like punishment than rewards. I was confident we could change how she felt about food. In fact, it is usually quite easy to reintroduce food as a reinforcer to a dog that has become turned off by it.

Management. This family couldn't control movement in their neighborhoods to accommodate their work with Dolly. We needed a backup plan: I told Mary if all else failed she could stand on Dolly's leash, close to the collar, so Dolly was at least prevented from jumping and biting at people.

Diet. We considered the possibility that Dolly didn't like the taste of her dry dog food. Mary decided to find another high caliber kibble she would like better. I recommended that instead of free feeding (leaving food out all day long), they should put food out two or three times a day, give her fifteen minutes with it, and remove what was uneaten. We hoped this, combined with the Super-Motivating treats, would build her interest in food.

Progress Reports from Family

Mary was good about letting me know how she and Dolly were doing with behavior modification and management. Over seven months, she reported the following:

Super-Motivating Treats: Initially, when Mary went through the whole procedure of cooking the chicken meatballs, Dolly wasn't interested in them. This is consistent with Mary's earlier assessment that Dolly was not treat-motivated. However, Mary persisted; when she cooked the treats a second time, Dolly was very interested in the treats. When Mary called "Chickie!", Dolly immediately let go of any interest and tuned in to the treats. Dogs that want something from us typically try to figure out how to get it. All Dolly had to do to get a "Chickie" was to let go of her interest in a trigger, for example a person, and follow the "Chickie" instead.

Neighborhood: Mary reminded me there was "a lot going on in the neighborhood this time of year. Many noises frighten Dolly and barking seems to be her fear reaction (sometimes the hair stands up on her neck)." Mary said she could "usually divert her with a treat or change of direction but if she can still hear the noise it takes time to calm her."

Neighbors as Allies: At first, neighbors forgot they weren't supposed to pet Dolly when they stopped to talk to Mary, and Mary had to step on Dolly's leash so she couldn't jump up and bite people. After a few weeks, most neighbors understood they could help Dolly if they ignored her and let Mary divert her attention with the squeaky toy, distance, and Super-Motivating treats.

Mary had to be vigilant. As Dolly's behavior improved, she could get closer to people without jumping up but she would lick them instead. Mary understood if she let this continue, Dolly would escalate to mouthiness and biting.

Mary also reported, "Seeing the neighbors on walks seems to have improved. If we're too close it works best if I keep her distracted with treats and as she lays down I step on the leash."

Meeting Dogs: Mary wrote, "Just yesterday we met a dog from the area that she'd seen once or twice before but not for a while. The owner was impressed by how confident Dolly was. He recalled that the last time they had met, she had been so fearful. The two dogs actually interacted a little."

Greetings: Within six weeks Dolly was "Much better with greetings. She looks the other way now for treats and the squeaky toy."

At three months Mary reported, "Dolly's doing well. It's still a little struggle with people entering the house and occasionally with someone on the street. However, it's much improved. The distraction works the best."

Six Months Progress Report

Update on Greetings: At six months Dolly was doing "very well. At home everything's great. Distraction works very well on the street. Sirens and other loud noises still scare her" but Mary could stop escalations. At this point Mary wanted to know, "How do I move to the next step of having people actually talk to her and pet her?"

Dolly was ready for greetings again. I suggested Mary let Dolly approach people and if she resorted to the old behaviors, Mary could intervene using the same protocols that worked so well during the transition months since the consult. I reiterated the key was to keep Dolly below threshold (before the point where she would rev up, bite and climb.)

I suggested that when people approach Dolly, it would help if they were low-key about it. In fact, they should try backing up to her, quietly, and later they could use frontal approaches. They should go slowly and ease Dolly into these greetings. If they can actually pet her without eliciting the old response, great!

About her in-home behavior, Mary reports, "Dolly now has free rein of the house. People come to greet her and she doesn't jump but will sit for a while. Sometimes she just sits beside me. She's definitely improved. Last month at the beach, what a difference! She used to be afraid just walking along; she was afraid of the ocean. Most often she's not jumping on us, though now and then, for some reason, she has a zoomy episode. This happens when she's tired and can't control herself. She's still upset by the sound of motorcycles. The Dramamine is working pretty well for car rides, she's not drooling like she used to." (Note: the Dramamine was recommended by Dolly's veterinarian.)

Notably, as Dolly's confidence grew, the submissive urination totally stopped. Mary said Dolly "seems like a different dog walking down the street. Her tail is up". No more wet greetings! She still encounters an occasional sight or sound that scares her, such as noisy carpet cleaners or a police car, but Mary knows how to handle her so Dolly's suffering is minimal.

Veterinary Visits: When Dolly saw her veterinarian for routine immunizations she did very well and the veterinarian commented she was pleased because Dolly was more relaxed and didn't ramp up during the visit.

Dog Food: Dolly's doing better with the (new food) recommended by her veterinarian. She doesn't dive in but eventually eats most of it.

Anti-Anxiety: The anxiety wrap, long strokes and music soothe Dolly at home and on long car rides.

Regular Harness: Mary reports, "The regular harness is so much more comfortable for Dolly. She runs much better with it."

Exercise Pen: Mary's relieved: "She's stopped climbing all over us. We took the x-pen down; we don't need it any more."

Perspective on Helping Dogs

Successful behavior management and modification have at their core a healthy respect for the dogs we have, not the dogs we wish for, not the dogs we encounter on our television screens, and not the dogs next door who never seem to do anything wrong. Most often our dogs with issues can't help themselves and they don't understand our negativity about their behavior. However, with empathy, imagination, and an educated understanding of the dogs we have, we can help so many of them.

As a reminder, dogs tell us by their behavior if we're moving too fast. It's far better to go too slow than to have to start over because we went too fast and our dogs fell off the reformation wagon.

Tucky's Pee Problems

Tucky is a twelve month-old, male, neutered, Shih Tzu weighing eight pounds. His person, Susan, told me by phone that the little guy has been causing big trouble in her house. He's peeing all over the place; she's "tried everything but nothing works".

The leading cause given by families for relinquishing their dogs to animal shelters is incomplete housetraining.[61] Small dogs are apt to fare better than big dogs with housetraining problems for the obvious reason that their output is comparatively small.

Small dogs appear to have more problems catching onto housetraining rules. Veterinary behaviorist Dr. Bonnie Beaver speculates that Toy breeds "were originally developed to retain the characteristics of puppies... (and) less desirable juvenile features (have been) retained. One of these is the resistance to being housebroken. In small dogs, housetraining can be a difficult, long-term problem."[62]

61   M. D. Salman, J. Hutchinson, R. Ruch-Gallie, et al. (2000). "Behavioral reasons for relinquishment of dogs and cats to 12 shelters". *Journal of Applied Animal Welfare Science*, 3 (2000): 93-106.

62   Bonnie Beaver, DVM, DACVB. *Canine Behavior: A Guide for Veterinarians* (W.B. Saunders Company, 1999).

Based on my experience with Toy dogs, I hypothesize they can be more difficult to housetrain for the following reasons:

- Toys dogs are more apt to have been trained initially to eliminate indoors and doing so becomes habit long before families try to transfer elimination outdoors. Thus, even when Toys eventually learn to eliminate outside, when they can't get there unimpeded, their memories of having eliminated indoors kicks in. Habit can carry them as follows (though not in any human language): "I've gotta' go, I need a place, can't get outside so I'll go in the living room instead. My people don't use that room much; it must be there for me." Alternatively, they might 'say' "I can't get outside so I'll just eliminate here by the door which is almost outside. Phew! What a relief."

- Toy dogs with thin coats are less protected from the elements. As such, they are less likely to brave cold, rain, sleet and snow.

- When the weather's bad, some Toys can be coaxed outside only if their owners go with them, but owners usually also want to avoid inclement weather. Thus, when dogs most need their family to face the elements with them, owners least want to offer their support. In other words, we (me included) become fair weather friends to our dogs. I don't mean this as a criticism of people (like me). After all, we are not the ones who must go outside to eliminate! If only we could offer our dogs flushable indoor toilets stationed in distant rooms. Imagine if we had such devices and dogs could only exit after flushing. As a finishing touch, a treat would automatically drop down to reward jobs well done!

- Finally, it's easier to clean up after Toys. The smaller the dog the less the output. As such, families with Toy dogs may be less vigilant about getting them outside.

History

Susan adopted Tucky when he was nine months old. From day one she tried to interest him in holding it until he got outdoors, whereas Tucky excelled at holding it until he got back in the house. Nature was not calling Tucky; grass was not his thing. He preferred absorbent surfaces such as carpets, draperies, and couches, but even a tile floor would do if he was in the kitchen and felt the urge.

Susan's attempts at problem-solving ranged from corrections ("no, no, no!"), to rejection ("get out of here you schmuck!"), lamentations ("how could you do this to me?), punishment (swats with a newspaper), admonishment ("bad, bad dog!"), threats ("if you do that again you're outta' here!"), confinement to a crate (he peed in the crate too), all of this intermingled with love and an "otherwise wonderful relationship."

I wasn't nearly as surprised as Susan to discover that none of her methods worked.

When Susan offered to adopt Tucky, she knew he had issues. His former family had spoken disparagingly about him in the community, telling others he was "incorrigible". They had "tried everything" but he wouldn't stop peeing in their house. After much effort, they gave up on him and sent him to their unfinished basement to live out his days, virtually alone. In exile, he was free to eliminate uninterrupted for a full month before Susan rescued him.

Susan had tremendous empathy for Tucky. She knew how it felt to be alone. She was still grieving from the sudden loss of her husband to a heart attack. Tucky was a friendly little fellow. Susan asked Tucky's captors if she could take him home to live with her. They warned, "He's not trainable. He'll pee all over your house too". Nevertheless, she brought him home, where he did exactly as they predicted.

Susan believed she could heal Tucky with her love, but while Tucky may have been lonely and desperate for empathy and attention, he couldn't be healed because he wasn't sick. Rather, he was a dog who had learned to eliminate inside, not outside, and his habits were now deeply ingrained.

TUCKY'S EARLY DEVELOPMENT SHOWS HOW ELIMINATION PATTERNS TOOK SHAPE

Birth to 10 weeks in a kennel. Tucky lived with his mother and two siblings in a kennel run that was comprised of a mix of tile and concrete flooring. The puppies eliminated freely in the run.

Research shows that puppies begin to establish location and surface preferences by 7 or 8 weeks.[63] Some conscientious breeders start training their puppies to eliminate outside on grass before they are adopted out. We can surmise from Tucky's behavior that he didn't have housetraining guidance during his weeks with the breeder.

10 weeks to 12 weeks in a cage. At 10 weeks the breeder dropped the puppies off at a pet store where they lived in a cage for two weeks. Tucky did all of his toileting in the cage or a play area that had a tile floor with some carpeting. It is not likely that he had ever in his lifetime been outdoors on grass.

AT 3 MONTHS ADOPTED BY FAMILY AND LIVED WITH THEM FOR 6 MONTHS

Tucky's family expected him to eliminate in their spacious fenced-in yard because that is what dogs do in yards. They knew from reading literature given to them at the pet store that he was old enough to hold it until he got outside. When they saw he was reluctant to even step outdoors, family members started going out with him. He didn't seem to know what to do with himself outside, though he did eventually learn to defecate (poop) in the yard. They couldn't tell when he eliminated because, as is common among young male dogs, he didn't lift his leg to pee. They took him out every couple of hours and after five or ten minutes brought him back inside where he did know very well how to deposit pee.

When Tucky's family caught him peeing in the house, they hit him with a newspaper, yelled, "No! Bad dog!" and whisked him outside. If they came home and saw he'd peed in the house, they brought him to the spot where the offense occurred, told him, "Bad, bad dog!" threatened him with a newspa-

....
63   J. P. Scott and J. L. Fuller. *Genetics and the Social Behavior of the Dog* (Chicago: University of Chicago Press, 1965).

per, and rubbed his nose in the spot. Animal behavior experts using modern techniques would not recommend any such interventions.

Within a few days, Tucky started running off to hide behind the couch when family members arrived home. They accepted this as proof the little fellow knew he had done wrong. They concluded he felt ashamed and guilty. As such, they continued punishing him for eliminating in the house. After a few weeks they discovered he was peeing behind the couch as well.

Challenged, the family decided to take Tucky for long walks around the neighborhood. He seemed to enjoy the walks and started peeing outside though he never really stopped peeing in the house. Even after peeing on walks, he would return home, sneak out of sight, and pee. The newspaper was brought out, "bad dog!" smack the dog, and the cycle continued.

Finally, as Tucky reached nine months of age, his family decided he was hopeless, and exiled him to the basement to live out his days. He was no longer welcome in the upstairs with the rest of his family.

Tucky moved in with Susan at nine months and continued the same patterns.

Assessing (Clueless) Tucky

Tucky has been out of sync with his people for most of his life. He eliminated whenever he felt the urge, on the surfaces available to him. His people got mad at him quite often and I doubt he ever knew why. He might have concluded that humans are irrational and unpredictable. Because he's a dog and rather friendly, he would love them anyway.

It's not unusual for dogs to go on long walks around the neighborhood and wait until they get home to eliminate. Veterinarian Dr. Ian Dunbar, one of the foremost trainers in the world, writes, "basically, there are three reasons why the dog would do this, as below.

Veterinarian Dr. Ian Dunbar on Why Dogs Wait 'Til They Return Indoors to Eliminate

The dog would much rather eliminate at home, in private.

> The dog has learned that its walk will end as soon as he has 'done his business'.
>
> The dog has learned that he must not eliminate in the presence of his people. [64]

We can surmise that Tucky is reluctant to eliminate when family are around because they've gotten mad at him in the past for doing so. He doesn't realize they're angry about his choice of spots, and that knowledge must perplex him: for his part, he would much rather eliminate inside the home because that is what he knows how to do best.

Families with dogs that are not completely housetrained often tell me, "He looks guilty, he obviously knows what he's done." I explain that he may accept their view of him as a "naughty boy" but not understand what he does that is bad.

Families are often convinced their dogs are "trying to get even" with them by staging misadventures. Anthropomorphizing can harm dogs in situations like this. Why assume our dogs know what we would know or feel in a similar situation? Tucky, for his part, clearly did not understand what it was about him that got his people upset. Nor did he understand the economics of the situation.

Think about it. How could he possibly know it costs money to replace carpets and furniture, and how could he know he has ruined them? They don't look ruined to him! Similarly, dogs don't know their humans could drop them off at a shelter and say "good riddance" whenever they feel like it, with minimal social repercussions. With absolutely no warning, families do drop dogs in dangerous situations and walk out of their lives forever.

Dogs, unlike some humans, do not seek revenge. As simple creatures, they concern themselves with toys, their next joyful greeting and their next meal.

Families also tell me, "He knows the meaning of 'No!' doesn't he?" Agreed, most dogs understand "no" but they don't easily connect with what, as in "no to what?" Tucky's conclusions might sound like this: "No, don't look happy when my family comes home" or "no, don't lift my leg" or "no, don't walk on the carpet" or "no,

....

64   Ian Dunbar, Ph.D.,, DVM, MRCVS. "Housetraining: Solve the Problem by Understanding the Process". <http://www.billfoundation.org/html/housetraining.html> . Additional articles and books by Dr. Dunbar are referenced in the Behavior Cache section under Puppy Tips .

don't sniff." It's much easier to teach dogs going forward, "yes, do this", than it is to teach dogs to think in reverse, "no, don't do that." Keep this in mind when you design any behavior modification plan for your dog.

Another point to consider is this: Families are apt to see their male dogs eliminate once and assume they are empty when they are not. Male dogs typically urinate three or more times to empty. Families need to know this so they don't bring their dogs inside prematurely.

Housetraining Essentials

Prevention: Allow No Mistakes. When we adopt puppies or dogs, we don't want bad habits to transfer to new homes. Our first resolve when bringing any dog home is to not give them opportunities to eliminate inside.

Back to the Basics. A good rule of thumb with dogs that are not reliably housetrained or are newly rehomed is to go back to housetraining basics. Start with the assumption that dogs new to homes need guidance on selecting human-preferred locations and surfaces for elimination.

Avoid Punishment. If we punish dogs for eliminating in our presence they may become averse to eliminating when we are around, even when we are outside with them on-leash. Tucky was punished and it didn't stop him from eliminating in the house; he adapted by finding out-of-the-way places to urinate. Punishment didn't teach him what he was supposed to do when he felt the urge.

Reward for Choosing the Right Locations and Surfaces. Families with new dogs should pick a general area where they want elimination to occur, take their dogs-in-training to that area, on-leash, and reward them when they use the area for its intended purpose. Dogs that are apprehensive about eliminating with their people around may require more freedom to choose their spot and surface. Outdoor surface preferences might be concrete, dirt or grass. Rewards might be treats, petting, scratching behind the ears, and happy voices.

Helping Tucky:
Behavior Management and Modification Plan

TEACHING TUCKY TO "GO" OUTSIDE

Choice of Reinforcers. I showed Susan how to create powerful reinforcers using the squeaky toy and the Super-Motivating treats to get Tucky's attention. (See instructions for "Super-Motivating Treats" in the "Behavior Cache" section). I wanted Tucky to begin to look to Susan for cues about what he should be doing and where, since it was clear we couldn't trust his judgment in these matters. Tucky might have learned as quickly if Susan had used a simple reinforcer such as a small training treat, but when dog's problems are so serious they threaten their survival in the home, why risk failure by using potentially weak reinforcers?

I offer one caveat to my advice about reinforcers: powerful rewards and owner excitement have the potential to stir up so much arousal that some dogs will neglect their need to eliminate and focus on getting good stuff from their person instead. I tone down to less interesting rewards for overenthusiastic dogs.

Susan agreed to take Tucky outside every few hours, on-leash, to an area in the yard where she wants him to eliminate. She also took him out after a nap (Tucky's nap, not Susan's!) and approximately twenty minutes after eating. She'd give him a command, "Hurry up!", and repeat the command, in a friendly way, if he eliminated outside. "Hurry up!" Just as he was finishing she would say "Good!" and offer him a "Chickie". I caution families, hold off on the reward until the dog is just finishing, to avoid interrupting the flow.

In hindsight, Tucky loved cooked chicken so much he would have been just as motivated by plain chicken. Chicken breast meat is easier to digest than many other foods such as cheese and it's low calorie, low fat, and an excellent source of protein. White skinless breast meat is less apt to cause digestive upset than brown meat from legs and thighs.

DETERRENTS TO ELIMINATING INSIDE

Thorough Cleaning to Minimize Odors. Susan agreed to deodorize all the areas where Tucky had eliminated in the house. Dogs are drawn to return to areas that have their or other dogs' scents and families would do well to clean these areas as thoroughly as possible. Black lights, moisture-detecting probes, and biological dyes can be used to find hidden urine spots. Most professional carpet and floor cleaners can handle pet elimination residues.

Putting Human Scent on Elimination Areas. As an extra measure, because Tucky tended to eliminate in out-of-the-way areas where humans didn't typically walk, Susan agreed to walk all over the clean, deodorized areas, barefoot. Some of her visiting friends and relatives did the same in an effort to communicate with Tucky in a language he would understand.

Putting Treats on Elimination Areas. Susan also put small training treats mixed with Tucky's dry dog food on the cleaned, dry and deodorized areas. Our goal was to communicate to Tucky that the "illegal" areas were not for peeing. Dogs don't understand our language as it concerns what we want from them and what might happen if they don't comply. Therefore, we must communicate in "language" they do understand.

Tethered but Free. After Tucky finished eliminating outside, Susan could let him run free in the house for up to an hour. Whenever he was loose in the house, a tether would be attached to his collar so Susan could gather him up for quick runs outside if she saw him start to sniff and circle, precursors to eliminating.

Tethered and Attached to Susan or Close to Susan. After the hour Tucky was free, Susan attached the tether either to herself or to nearby furniture or doors so he would always be within arm's reach for quick flights outside and he couldn't sneak off to eliminate. If she couldn't supervise him on the tether, Susan would confine him to a small crate that was "clean", i.e., he had not eliminated in this crate before. He didn't eliminate in the new crate because it was a sleeping area. He couldn't be in larger crates because he had experience eliminating in those, just beyond the space where he slept. He learned to eliminate in contained areas during his weeks in a cage at the pet store, and his months before that in the kennel with his litter.

When Susan took Tucky along to visit relatives and friends they would go on long walks beforehand so he'd arrive empty. She then kept him tethered to her so he wouldn't have the opportunity to eliminate in other people's houses.

As a further deterrent, when she couldn't supervise as closely, she took the additional precaution of putting a Belly Band around Tucky, made especially for male dogs.[65] It can take several weeks for dogs to adjust to belly bands. (Warning: Supervision is required.)

DIET

Susan reported Tucky occasionally had diarrhea. A routine veterinary check didn't turn up any problems. He was eating grocery store kibble. I suggested Susan discuss nutrition with her veterinarian with the goal of changing him to one of the high-rated foods. With the better foods Tucky might enjoy better long-term health with the side benefit that his stools would be smaller and firmer. (See "Finding Top Foods" in the "Behavior Cache" section for links to reliable information on dog foods.)

Susan left food out in one bowl all day for Tucky to eat whenever he wanted. I suggested she feed him just twice a day. She agreed to put the food out in a dish, give him fifteen minutes or so to eat, and then remove it until his next meal. Having food available all the time makes elimination less predictable. In addition, we wanted to use food as a reinforcer and Tucky was not as interested in food because it was always available.

POSITIVE ATTENTION FOR ELIMINATING OUTSIDE

Tucky was used to getting quite a lot of attention for peeing in the house, and dogs learn that even negative attention has it's rewards. When dog's owners are angry with them, the paradox is they need even more reassurance in the form of attention. I asked Susan to give Tucky lots of attention inside when he was just hanging out, and outside when he eliminated.

WHEN OWNERS ARE GONE FOR LONG STRETCHES

Some families put newspaper out or expect their dogs to use a litter box designed for canines. The litter boxes can be a tough sell; dogs on their own

---

65 Search for belly bands at <http://www.amazon.com>.

don't choose to eliminate in small areas with sides all around. Newspaper can become soggy, smelly and shredded. For puppies, families that are gone for long stretches can link several interlocking crates together and put "grass" (synthetic grasses scented for dogs, or sod with grass made for this purpose) in one crate for eliminating. You may have to look online for interlocking crates. This option can work for families who want their dogs to eliminate outside when they get a little older. Dogs don't learn location this way but they do develop surface, or substrate, preferences for grass.

It's not wise to leave puppies or dogs home alone for such long periods they are forced to eliminate in their crates or other areas where they are confined, such as a kitchen or basement—unless families leave a "legal" area in their crate system or other confinement area where they can eliminate freely. Dogs forced to adjust to soiled crates or other areas develop "bad" habits that bring them into conflict with their humans when they get bigger.

Some owners install dog doors and fences around yards so dogs can go out to eliminate whenever they want.

When taking dogs outside to eliminate, give them about five minutes. If they go, reward them with favored reinforcers. If they don't go, return to the house and keep them tethered and supervised or in a crate or other confined, low-stress area. Take them out an hour or so later if they didn't empty when given opportunities.

Keep in mind that if you take some dogs out too often, they never learn to "hold it". It this is happening with your dog, consider keeping him tethered to you inside for longer stretches and take him out every two hours or longer, instead of every hour.

Male dogs that aren't neutered tend to have more problems with soiling in the house. Some breeds have a higher incidence of house soiling problems and some dogs are naturally more difficult to housetrain.[66] Dogs with separation anxiety might eliminate inside when they are home alone; similarly, some dogs offer "wet" greetings when they are excited.

....
66 W. E. Campbell. "Which dog breeds develop what behavioral problems?", *Modern Veterinary Practice*. (1972): 53:31.

If a dog manages to pee outside and only defecates in the house, with some consistency, consider that the dog might not be staying outside long enough to empty both ways. Dogs might be in a rush to get back inside because they are afraid of what's out there. For example, they might worry about an electronic containment system that, in their estimation, has "bitten" them in the past. Families with worried dogs might have to go outside with them to ensure they empty. Some families end up dismantling electronic systems and installing real fences or using leashes for the duration. I don't know how many families use electronic containment systems successfully. I'm a trouble-shooter; most of the dogs I encounter in my practice have problems with them.

Progress Report for Tucky

Tucky quickly learned to "hold it" inside and to eliminate outside on the grass. He was entranced by the Super-Motivating treats, fun squeaks from the toy, and Susan's exuberance when they were outside together. Per Susan's report one month later, Tucky's problem had completely resolved. Susan said she couldn't have asked for a better relationship with a dog than the one she had with Tucky after the source of conflict between them was vanquished.

Indoor Elimination Systems

Our other option would have been to use one of the indoor elimination systems that work so well for some Toy dogs. The Pup-Head™ Portable Dog Potty, by PupGear Corporation, is one example. I have four clients who used the Pup-Head successfully, one on their sailboat.[67] The challenge is teaching dogs to use it.

Amazon.com carries a product that works for one client with a Toy poodle. It's called UGODOG Indoor Dog Potty.[68] Read the reviews to understand

----

67 PupGear, <http://www.portabledogpotty.com>. Their advertising reads as follows: Pup-Head"! is a perfect solution for apartments, high-rise buildings, boats, or recreational vehicles and great during inclement weather. Perfect for pet owners with busy or unpredictable schedules as well as those who are elderly or handicapped

68 UGODOG Indoor Dog Potty, <http://www.amazon.com>.

the pros and cons on this and other products. Read also about Pup-Grass, a synthetic grass for dogs.[69]

Another product that has received positive reviews from clients is the PETaPOTTY and the Marathon Lite Sod that is sold with it, or separately[70]. The prime advantages to the soilless sod are, it's real grass and yet doesn't leave a mess. It may hold up for several months if properly cared for. I've used the Marathon Lite Sod successfully to change dog's substrate preference from concrete in kennel runs to grass.

Families with cats report one of the prime advantages is that cats eliminate in litter boxes and can take care of their own needs when nature calls. Unless we have dog doors that enable dogs to go in and out at will, dogs depend on us to gain access to yards. Families have to be like United States Postal Service mail persons and deliver their dogs to legal outdoor spots, through rain, wind, sleet, snow, and even avalanches, hurricanes and earthquakes. Think about it. I know of Toy dog owners who circumvent the whole problem by adapting their dogs from the outset to indoor or porch-based potty systems. In the dead of winter, when I have to shovel snow to create pathways for pooches, I've wished I'd done the same.

....

69   Pup-Grass, <http://www.pup-grass.com>.
70   PETaPOTTY , <http://www.petapotty.com>.

Maggie's Awakening

In the story that follows, Maggie's caretaker, Carole, intuited her way to a creative solution to a troubled dog's problems. When confronted with challenging behavior problems we have to experiment to discover what rewards will make the best positive reinforcers and what interventions will yield the best results for the dog we have. Our behavior modification and management plans must be individualized, or tailored to the dog at-hand, and not administered cookie-cutter style. Going cookie-cutter will yield about the same results as cherry picking ideas: no significant change.

Carole Duffy is a retired Pittsburgh mounted patrol officer. She told me she agreed to care for a neighbor's dog, an eight-month old Border collie, Maggie, while the neighbor went to a funeral out-of-state. The neighbor assured Carole her adolescent dog was fully house-trained, "most of the time." She dropped Maggie and a dog crate off at Carole's front door around bedtime and instructed Carole to have Maggie sleep in the crate at night and when Carole was not home. The neighbor drove off, rather quickly as Carole recalls.

Within two minutes in Carole's house, Maggie peed in her family room. Carole took her for a long walk but Maggie didn't urinate or defecate until she got back to Carole's house. She urinated again when she was on her back, while Carole was grooming her. Carole cleaned up and put her in her crate because it was time for bed.

Within seconds Maggie peed in the crate and scratched and splashed as she did every time she relieved herself in the wrong place. This made quite a mess. Throughout the night and in the morning, after her walk, she made more messes in the house, always with the scratching and splashing as a finale.

It's obvious from her behavior that Maggie was not housetrained and she was used to eliminating in her crate. Dogs are simple. They show us what their experience has been, with no covering-up to make things look better or worse than they are. Since she did eliminate once while being groomed, we can surmise she felt some anxiety over being in a stranger's home or anxiety over being handled, but anxiety alone would not have led her to such behavioral extremes.

Carole discovered by asking around that Maggie's person went off to work and left Maggie in the crate all day, for eight to ten hours. Let's not skirt around the issue: Maggie was being warehoused and she wasn't housetrained. She spent most of her time, day and night, in a crate. Border collies are usually high energy, quick learners and must have a job and other environmental stimulation to keep them happy. Border collies and similar breeds especially need movement. For Maggie, relegation to a crate for such long hours constituted abuse.

The indoor habit must have been deeply ingrained because nothing Carole did helped. Maggie kept eliminating in her house. By the third night, Carole was ready to try something new. She had a lifetime of experience bonding with animals and understood that getting animals into a right relationship with their humans can make a difference.

Carole did something simple and bold that changed the structure of the relationship and yielded dramatic results: Carole decided not to use the crate any more. She invited Maggie to instead sleep on her bed. That night, for the first time, Maggie cuddled next to Carole and didn't eliminate in the house.

The next morning, after Maggie eliminated outside, Carole took her experiment further: she traveled with Maggie to a nearby farm that has sheep, and then to a horse farm to meet Carole's horse and partner, Donald Duck who, like Carole, was retired from Pittsburgh's police force. Maggie was intensely interested in the sheep. She crouched low and eyed them, as Border collies do. Later, she touched noses with Donald Duck and paid rapt attention when the horses were turned out to pasture. Throughout the day she eliminated outside, naturally; Carole reinforced her with praise and training treats.

After the night of freedom and companionship and an adventure-filled day,

Maggie didn't eliminate in Carole's house ever again. When the neighbor returned from her trip, Carole told her what happened and gave her an article about Border Collies' personalities and drives. The neighbor wasn't happy (she had to pay for carpet cleaning) and didn't admit to anything, but Carole heard several months later that Maggie had been sent to live with a farmer with cows—and after learning she could only interact with the cows if she was gentle with them, he let her herd them!

Separation Distress

Most of us know of dogs that never miss an opportunity to get into mischief when they are home alone and free to roam. Many dogs can't handle such freedoms before eighteen months to two-and-a-half years and longer for really late-bloomers. On the other end of the continuum of dogs who "make trouble" when they are left behind are the ones whose destructiveness attests to a frantic desperation. These dogs can barely tolerate their circumstances, and it shows.

Dogs overly stressed by separations leave telltale signs such as scratched doors and chewed doorknobs, ripped and chewed furniture and carpets, urination and defecation (by otherwise housetrained, physically healthy dogs), or vomiting. Dogs confined to steel crates have been known to break their teeth, bloody paws and destroy bedding while trying to escape.

The severity of the damage attests to the intensity of their distress. Other signs are barking or howling, refusals to eat even the best of foods, drooling, attention-seeking leading up to departures, and even occasional reports of aggression from dogs seeking to stop their humans from walking out the door.

Dogs that enjoy good-enough relationships with their human families typically want to spend as much time as they can with them. Steven Lindsay wrote in his *Handbook of Applied Dog Behavior and Training: Procedures and Protocols*, "When left alone, all normal dogs appear to experience some degree of discomfort by separation; however, the vast majority learns to cope with routine separation without becoming overly distressed. Many, though, respond adversely to separation, exhibiting varying degrees of despair, emotional arousal, or panic."[71]

Contributing factors to separation distress are anxiety, boredom, fear, stress, frustration, and panic.[72]

When I get a call about a dog that appears to have issues with separation, I respond quickly. Too often, the dogs are suffering acutely and so are their families. The problem is always challenging, more so when humans must be away from home for full days, all week long. It must be understood, however, that some dogs show signs of separation distress when their humans are at home and they're confined to a space such as their crate.[73] Initial symptoms can surface when humans return to work or school after taking time off. As such, any dramatic, extreme changes in schedule can result in separation distress.[74]

Below are links to information about separation anxiety on the Internet. If this is an area of interest, I encourage you to read the articles and view the videos on the Applied Ethology Web site.[75] Ethology is the "study of animal behavior with emphasis on the behavioral patterns that occur in natural environments."[76]

Where to Find Reliable Information on Separation Distress

- "Separation Anxiety in Dogs: bibliographies, Web sites, and resources". University of California Davis (UC Davis), Veterinary Medicine, Center for Companion Animal Health, www.vetmed.ucdavis.edu/CCAB/separation.html.

- "Separation Anxiety in Dogs", article and video clips.

71   Steven Lindsay. (2005) *Applied Dog Behavior and Training: Volume 3: Procedures and Protocols* (Blackwell Publishing, 2005). 182.

72   Steven Lindsay and Victoria Lea Voith. (2000) *Applied Dog Behavior and Training: Volume 1: Adaptation and Learning*. (Blackwell Publishing, 2000). Ch. 4, Separation Distress and Coactive Influences .

73   V. L. Voith, P. L. Borchelt. "Separation anxiety in dogs. The Compendium on Continuing Education for the Practicing Veterinarian". 7(1) (1985): 42

74   E A. McCrave. "Diagnostic criteria of separation anxiety in the dog". *Veterinary Clinics of North America, Small Animal Practice*, 21(2) (1991): 247-55

75   *Applied Ethology,* <http://www.usask.ca/wcvm/herdmed/applied-ethology/>.

76   *Random House Dictionary*, s.v. ethology <http://www.dictionary.com>.

- Applied Ethology, www.usask.ca/wcvm/herdmed/applied-ethology/behaviourproblems/anxiety.html.

- DVM360, *DVM Newsmagazine* (Veterinary Medicine).

- Search DVM360.com for articles using term "separation anxiety", www.dvm360.com.

- Separation Anxiety". www.marvistavet.com/html/body_separation_anxiety.html.

- "Separation Anxiety in Dogs" article by Debra Horwitz, DVM, DACVB, a veterinary behaviorist in St. Louis, Missouri, and president of the American College of Veterinary Behaviorists. To read on the Internet, go to www.vetmedicine.about.com/ and type the title of the article in the search box.

Relationship Risk Factors: Attachment Issues

Research shows that dogs with separation anxiety are three times as likely to have come from an animal shelter as are dogs with other problems.[77] Most of the dogs I've worked with that have separation issues were adopted from shelters. We don't know if their families relinquished them because they were symptomatic, or if the dogs developed separation issues because of instability and abandonment in earlier relationships with their humans. Shelters don't often get the straight scoop on relinquished dogs.

Conversely, Flannigan and Dodman researched the potential risk factors and behaviors associated with separation anxiety by comparing the medical records of 200 separation anxious dogs with 200 control dogs. Results showed that dogs "from a home with a single adult human were approximately 2.5 times as likely to have separation anxiety as dogs from multiple owner homes, and sexually intact dogs were a third as likely to have separation anxiety as neutered dogs. Several factors associated with hyper attachment to the owner were significantly associated with separation anxiety. Significantly, spoiling activities, sex of the dog, and the presence of other pets in the home were

---

77   V. L. Voith and D. Ganster. "Separation anxiety: Review of 42 cases". *Applied Animal Behavior Science*, 37 (1993): 84-85.

not (my emphasis) associated with separation anxiety . . . Hyper attachment to the owner was significantly associated with separation anxiety; extreme following of the owner, departure cue anxiety, and excessive greeting that may help clinicians distinguish between canine separation anxiety and other separation-related problems." In addition, "results don't support the theory that early separation from the (mother) leads to future development of separation anxiety."[78]

Managing Togetherness Forces

When we set out to modify problem behaviors, one relationship variable we can manipulate is interpersonal distance. It's something I experiment with during consults: when we increase or decrease the emotional and/or physical distance between dogs and their humans, how does behavior change? Similarly, how do we maintain healthy boundaries and yet enjoy close, reciprocal relationships with our dogs?

Individual dogs have varying needs for companionship, as do their humans. One of my clients shared an interesting insight with me about her family's devoted Doberman pinscher. At night, he preferred sleeping in his crate in the basement, far from his people. Though he was not aggressive to strangers, he did spend his days and evenings on patrol, checking to see that his family was safe and secure. The nighttime arrangement seemed to give him relief because he was finally "off duty" and could get some real rest. He welcomed his time alone.

Other dogs flourish when they can be with their families as often as possible, and especially through the night. Sleeping in their human's bedrooms can strengthen bonds. Most dogs accept invitations to sleep on their human's beds or don't wait for an invitation.

It's true that some dogs cannot handle bed privileges and we have to establish different rules for them. For example, dogs that persist at growling at a spouse, or dogs that get huffy when their humans move around in bed, may

----

78   G. Flannigan, DVM, MSc and N. H. Dodman, BVMS, DACVB. "Risk factors and behaviors associated with separation anxiety in dogs". *Journal of the American Veterinary Medical Association*, 219(4) (Aug 15, 2001): 460-66.

not be good candidates for shared-bed privileges. If they complain and we have to eject them, thirty seconds on the floor is enough to convince some dogs that their humans will decide what privileges they get and they can't get preferred privileges on demand.

Dogs whose behavior cannot be quickly modified may require more elaborate plans that enable humans to establish their governance of the bed but do not put themselves in direct conflict with their dogs. For example, they can establish an even "sweeter", more appealing spot off the bed and lure the dog to that repeatedly. In addition, they can put barriers around the bed, using a combination of furniture, baby gates, crates. Why fight when luring and blocking are effective and are apt to yield good long-term results?

When Separation Rocks!

When we want to prevent or modify separation anxiety, we would do well to think about relationship variables that increase interpersonal distance. What causes dogs to feel joy or relief over their human's departures? I hope these examples make you laugh; they are meant to be funny but truthful:

Dogs that raid trash cans as a hobby are apt to appreciate when careless humans run out the door and leave accessible trash cans in their wake; similarly, counter surfers would be darned pleased to find dinner sitting on a counter, unguarded.

Most dogs don't enjoy having their ears cleaned and are happy for interruptions of that procedure. If their humans suddenly drop what they are doing and rush off, some dogs undoubtedly experience separation relief and even some joy over their sudden departure.

Having toenails clipped tends to be low on the scale of enjoyable activities that dogs share with their humans. Imagine how some dogs feel when their humans take off just after nail #1 is clipped, but before the dreaded clippers arrive at nail #2.

Dogs don't typically enjoy baths and some try to run away from home after a bath. Imagine how dogs resigned to their fate feel when their humans get them in the tub and then release them without the bath because they realize they are late for an appointment.

Opportunity knocks for dogs that are tightly bonded with one human when the spouse or significant other travels out-of-town. The dogs have their special person to themselves for a few days and attachments can become significantly stronger, to the point where we might say the dogs have become "hyper-attached". This might be evidenced by the dog's distress over separations from their special person. When the spouse returns, the dogs aren't happy to see them and the relationship with their special person loses some intensity. The separation issues dissipate, however.

I don't recommend owners "treat" separation anxiety by making nuisances of themselves. On the other hand, in the course of a day we naturally add touches of unpleasantness to the mix of emotional forces. We might rush through the house and narrowly miss tripping over a dog, inadvertently slam a door, fail to accidently drop food on the floor for them to eat, raise our voice, let the phone ring too long, and try to clean their ears. It's a hard knocks life. We might suppose that dogs can develop problems with separation if boundaries are not created in the natural course of their lives.

Cassie's Salvation

Cassie is a thirty-five pound, three year-old spayed female Spaniel mix, adopted from a shelter by Janet, a single woman who works long hours away from home. Janet got Cassie to keep a beloved Greyhound company. The two dogs got along and Cassie bonded quickly and sweetly to Janet, but when Janet was gone Cassie chewed, gnawed and destroyed doors, walls, carpeting, and furniture. In addition, Cassie panicked during thunderstorms and caused further damage when she tried to escape. Janet's father complained when he had to drive in from out-of-state to replace drywall and repair other damage. He pressured her to "get rid of the dog". Cleaning up after Cassie was getting expensive and there was no end in sight.

Role of Veterinarian

ASSESS FOR MEDICAL PROBLEMS

Results from blood work, a urine culture and urinalysis were negative. The veterinarian diagnosed Cassie as having separation anxiety and assessed she likely did not have an underlying medical disorder. She prescribed anti-anxiety medications known to help some dogs with separation distress and referred Janet to me for a behavior plan.

PRESCRIBE MEDICATIONS AS INDICATED

Most of us have mixed feelings about giving dogs psychotropic medications to reduce anxiety. Medications have unexpected side effects, they can be expensive (it pays to shop around!), and it can be a struggle to get the dosage right. Some families complain that medications make their dogs feel groggy and disconnected, a shell of their former selves. In addition, they can ease suffering for a while and then stop working, unpredictably.

On the other hand, separation anxiety is such a challenge because dogs are frantic when their humans are not on hand to guide and comfort them. Anyone who has seen a dog in acute distress over separations will tell you, it's painful to watch. Some families consider euthanasia as a desperate measure to end their dog's suffering.

In my experience, dogs with significant anxiety typically respond better to behavioral interventions when they are medicated. Medicating is something concrete that veterinarians can facilitate to immediately reduce suffering and buy families time. Medications applied in combination with the natural relaxers can take the edge off, enough for some at-risk dogs to remain in their homes.

There are occasional veterinarians who turn down client requests for psychotropic medications because they "don't believe in" them. If in doubt about your veterinarian's stance on medicating for separation anxiety, you might want to ask office staff before scheduling an appointment so you don't end up paying for an unproductive visit, and your dog is not left to suffer.

Another option is to ask your veterinarian to work in concert with a veterinary behaviorist who would be available for a telephone consult focused on your dog. There are veterinary behaviorists who provide this service from a distance as an assist to veterinarians trying to help dogs with issues. The cost can be surprisingly reasonable. You might be able to schedule a conference call between you, the veterinary behaviorist and your veterinarian. If you don't have conferencing capabilities, you can use one of the free conference call services on the Internet. (I have used both www.freeconferencecall.com and www.freeconference.com successfully.)

CASSIE'S VETERINARIAN

Janet was referred to me by Cassie's veterinarian, who put Cassie on anti-anxiety medications starting two weeks before my consult. Janet and I worked out a behavior modification plan that fit with Janet's capabilities. She agreed to take Cassie to daycare two days a week, on Tuesdays and Thursdays. This left Cassie with three days to be home without Janet.

Cassie responded reasonably well to the behavior interventions and had a good first week. She loved playing with the dogs at daycare and came home exhausted. The next day she was tired and this helped her though the days alone. However, mid-way through her second week Cassie's symptoms returned full force. She had diarrhea as a symptom of a bacterial infection and her veterinarian hypothesized that the medications were washing out of her system. Janet couldn't bear knowing Cassie was suffering acutely. Her house sustained new damage, and she again considered euthanasia as a way out.

Research shows that "most owners are glad they made the effort to try to help their pet, yet only 46% report an overall success rate of 80-100%."[79]. Janet's weekday work schedule couldn't be altered. The risk to Cassie was great. I suspected we could again make progress but we'd always have backsliding and at some point Janet would give up and Cassie would be gone.

Rehoming as an Intervention

I talked to Janet about finding a surrogate "Mom" who could be there for

79   Beaver, *Canine Behavior,* 260. See also Voith and Ganster. "Separation anxiety: Review of 42 cases", 84-85.

Cassie in a way Janet could not. Janet sensed we were approaching the end of the line and set out to rehome Cassie. She looked for a special someone who had control over their schedule, could be home often, and was willing to carry out a behavior modification and management plan. Janet committed to paying for the medications for as long as necessary and she would take Cassie back at any time if a new owner couldn't stay with it.

Several adopters expressed an interest in Cassie but were put off by her issues. We didn't have to wait long before a trusted relative stepped up to the plate, however. An aunt had an illness that was not life-threatening but usually kept her at home. Cassie had visited the aunt before and played happily with her and her dogs. The aunt agreed to carry out the plan to modify Cassie's response to separations with all of us hoping she would improve over time.

The aunt experienced some success with Cassie and offered her a permanent home. One year later the aunt had to be hospitalized and Janet brought Cassie and the other dogs to her house, temporarily. Janet followed the protocols we established earlier and Cassie's separation issues didn't resurface. When the aunt was released from the hospital and able to get around, Cassie went back to live with her with no apparent negative effects. Cassie remained bonded both with the aunt and with Janet.

Rehoming is a viable option for dogs whose needs can be met as well or better in a new home, especially if they bond with relative ease.

I wish we could build networks of "safe houses" in communities with surrogate moms and dads willing to lend dogs a hand during their time of need. Americans are graying, meaning there will be more citizens in their retirement years than ever before and they could step in to smooth dog's passages. Why not create safe houses in our communities to help dogs along?

Punishment Hurts

When owners come home and encounter destruction of property and messiness, they might think their dogs intentionally misbehaved and reprimand them for making a mess of things. The dogs, for their part, look suitably guilty, as if they "know what they've done". In truth, all these dogs are likely to know is that their humans are upset with them and they feel bad about it. We might surmise that punishment upon return of owners is undermining; it renders anxious dogs even less capable of handling their environment.

Boundaries/ Interpersonal Distance

When dogs with separation issues come to us for attention perhaps that is what they need and we should give it to them. However, if the humans involved have been consistently attentive, I might encourage them to change direction and increase interpersonal distance to see if that helps. For example, when humans are home they might busy themselves, move quickly from room to room, try to catch up on housework, and not stop often to tend to their dog. They aren't unpleasant with their dogs; they just tune in less, and especially let go if the dogs engage in other activities that occupy their attention. We do the same for our growing children.

Increasing interpersonal distance to create boundaries, if used, would be a small part of any plan. To help Cassie, the aunt was there for her but didn't pay much attention to her. The aunt noted Cassie would then go off and pester the other dogs to play with her. Increasing interpersonal distance gave us an edge in helping Cassie channel her anxiety.

I don't usually recommend that separation anxious dogs be banished from bedrooms, though there is occasionally a compelling reason to do so. For example, a Yorkshire terrier with mild separation issues was also growling at the family from her "throne" on the bed and putting her on the floor for a minute didn't help. For her, we set up barriers so she could be in the room with her humans but would not have access to the bed. After a week her humans let her up on the bed again and she did not resume growling. The behavior resurfaced months later and the family simply went back to using the barriers for a short while and again succeeded in extinguishing the behavior.

Relaxation Strategies

I always recommend that medications prescribed by the dog's veterinarian be combined with use of the natural relaxers. Most clients want to use them all: soothing music, anxiety wraps, massage, and relaxation exercises. (I discussed how to use these strategies and some limitations in detail in the "Dolly" section.) As a reminder, the secret to success with relaxers is to introduce the various devices when the dog is already relaxed and nothing else is going on. We want relaxation as a conditioned response; dogs relax more if they are accustomed to relaxing to stimuli. We can then ease into using the relaxers in higher stress situations.

Diet

Janet was inadvertently feeding Cassie a low-caliber dry dog food manufactured by a company with wide-ranging marketing campaigns. I've seen a correlation between nutrition and reactivity in dogs. I have encountered variations in temperament in my own dogs when I changed their foods.

Recently, my Yorkie became irritable and snappy when I added a high-caliber canned food to his dry food for flavoring. When I used chicken breast meat instead, the irritability vanished. When I tried this sequence again I got the same results and surmised the canned food was causing the problem. When I switched to a different high-caliber canned food he was fine, however.

We know from our own lives that good nutrition supports long-term good health. I recommended Janet review the most recent list of top dry dog foods, and the article on selection criteria, from the Whole Dog Journal[80] and visit Consumer Search[81] and then discuss the possibilities with her veterinarian. Having worked with Cassie's veterinarian for years, I knew I could count on her to recommend only the top quality dog foods.

Preparing to Leave

Our dogs typically are alert to signs we're leaving. They know if we leave at the same time every day, wear familiar clothing, complete the same last-minute chores, and pick up our keys and head for the door. Behaviorists call these "pre-departure cues". Some separation anxious dogs become distressed when they see these pre-departure cues, long before we actually walk out the door.

---

80 Whole Dog Journal, <http://www.whole-dog-journal.com>.
81 Consumer Search, <http://www.consumersearch.com/dog-food>.

Anticipatory Arousal

If "anticipatory arousal" is an issue for your dog–that is, if your dog becomes anxious and upset when he or she sees you prepare to leave the house, you may help if you change the typical cues leading up to your departure. For example:

- Ignore your dog for about a half hour before you leave.

- Once you have chosen a suitable confinement area, you can put your dog in the area a few minutes before you leave.

- You can follow the familiar preparations but change the ending: For example, instead of going out the door and leaving the dog behind at the regular time, you could invite your dog to come along on a fun trip such as a drive to the park. This helps transform some dog's feelings about pre-departure cues, from worry to hope and happy expectation.

- You can intersperse departure cues with other activities that are fun for your dog. For example, get dressed for work or school, grab a quick breakfast, pick up the keys . . . then play tug or throw a ball for your dog to chase before you walk out the door.

- You can proceed with the standard preparations, pick up the keys, walk out the door, shut it, then immediately open the door again and return to the house.

- You can change the order of preparations. For example, pick up your keys, walk out the door, start the car, come back in and eat breakfast, then finish dressing and leave, without any fanfare.

- Just before leaving, you could confine your dog while you create a trail made from pieces of Super-Motivating treats, and then release your dog to follow the trail to "Chickies!" as you walk out the door. At first, return quickly but build up to leaving for longer periods of time. Cassie, who had a robust appetite and managed to eat on all but her worst days alone, especially loved this intervention with the trail of treats. After a few weeks she wanted her new special person, the aunt, to leave so she could go on a "Chickie Hunt". This can be impossible to carry off successfully when there are multiple dogs, all wanting "Chickies". The aunt put her other dogs in a separate room so Cassie wouldn't have to compete for "Chickies".

- Turn on the radio or television first thing in the morning and leave it on when you depart, or play soothing music.

- Practice graduated departures[82] involving progressively longer and more realistic departure exposures.

Some dogs don't become upset until we're gone for a while. If your dog is not bothered by the expectation that you are about to leave, pre-departure cues don't matter. Save your energy for the interventions that are better matched to your dog's needs.

Start with Brief Separations

Try getting ready to leave, walk out the door, shut it, and then come back inside. Initially, return immediately and build up to staying away fifteen seconds, then 30 seconds, a minute, three minutes, five minutes, fifteen minutes.

Similarly, when you have built up to leaving for five minutes or so and your dog is tolerating that well, you can start the car and then, instead of driving off, return to the house.

Coming Home

Home at Last! When you walk in the door, look the other way, disinterested, busy with other things until your dog is calm. Be purposefully boring. As always, don't punish dogs for what they did while you were away.

----

82   Voith and Ganster. "Separation anxiety: Review of 42 cases", 42.

Where to Leave Separation Distressed Dogs When Staying Home is Not an Option

Try not to leave the dog in some out of the way place like the basement, or another location they would consider unpleasant, or aversive.

Separation anxious dogs generally don't hold up well in crates and they can break teeth and bloody paws trying to escape. So, don't crate your dog—unless you have a rare separation anxious dog that derives comfort from his crate!

There are always exceptions. I've had success with a few dogs where crating was the only option, using the "Create a Wonderland in the Crate" approach that is described below. It's designed to help dogs change how they feel about confinement.

Creating a Wonderland in a Crate

- The crate should have interior cushioning that makes it soft and comfortable, a prime spot for a snooze. Do the best you can with this. Some anxious dogs rip their cushioning to shreds and they could harm themselves by ingesting pieces of it.

- Positive reinforcers, or rewards such as Super-Motivating treats, stuffed Kongs, favored stuffed and squeaky toys, should be put in the crate, with the crate door left open.

- Put your dog's meals in the crate. If pieces are sprinkled around dogs have something to do, searching for all the pieces. Dogs start to view the crate as a source of nurturance and fun.

- Gradually you will be able to shut the door for a brief time, initially no more than a minute. Always try to release the dog before he becomes more than minimally anxious or stressed over his confinement.

- Relaxation strategies, such as soothing music, anxiety wraps and dog appeasing pheromones, should be employed. You are going for maximum relaxation in the crate.

- Go slowly, but not so slowly your dog simply adapts to having all of these goodies and to top it off, you too! Your dog has to let go of you, if only a little at first, to get the other good stuff.

- Increase the time the dog is in the crate with the door closed and family nearby. Leave the room for a few minutes. Build up to leaving the house briefly and leaving for longer stretches.

- At the outset, dogs will polish off the goodies in their crate and ask to get out. After a while, they grow to like their crates. Now it's time to change directions and put something super-motivating in the crate, such as fresh-cooked hot dog bits or Super-Motivating treats, but shut the door to keep the dog out. Now the dog must work to get *in* the crate.

- Some dogs will work as hard to get in as they used to work to get out of crates. Open the door and let the dog in.

- From now on, you plant positive reinforcers in the crate but don't open the door until you are ready to walk out of the room. You swing the crate door open, leave, and he gets the rewards!

- Build up to stocking the crate, lock the dog out, open the crate door, dog goes in, you lock the crate door and walk out of the room and then out of the house...for short periods and then longer periods. As always, listen for feedback from your dog. Dogs let us know if we're going too fast or the complete wrong way. If we make zero progress, we're going too slow or have selected the wrong interventions. Their behavior needs to change, if only slightly at the various stages.

- *Reminder:* Medications may still provide the real salvation unless your dog's separation anxiety is mild. If you try the above protocols and fail, it will be hard for you to introduce them in the future and succeed. These are reasons to work with a qualified professional, though it's a challenge to find one in many communities. I do what I can to maximize my chances of success the first time around, so no intervention is wasted. As such, I prefer having more than mildly separation distressed dogs on medications prescribed by their veterinarian.

- As alternatives to crates, you can try putting up baby gates and dog exercise pens. Some of my clients succeeded when they tied interesting objects to areas where destruction occurs, such as doors, and got the dogs interested in interacting with the objects.

Muzzles

While I don't recommend leaving muzzles on dogs when you are not there to supervise, some of my client families have successfully muzzled their separation anxious dogs to protect their dogs and their property, and this management tool has given them enough respite to keep the dogs in their homes while they carry out behavior modification plans. (See "Muzzles" in the "Behavior Cache" section for instructions on how to introduce muzzles.)

Role of Exercise

Some dogs, such as Dolly, become more frazzled when they are tired. However, exercise has a calming effect on most dogs. You can combine this with other strategies aimed at modifying behaviors. For example, you can get yourself ready to go out the door but, instead of leaving, you invite your dog to come along and drive him to a fun place where he can run around. Dogs get more exercise and possibly better relaxation when they are on flexi-leashes or long leads, than when they are contained on a regular-sized (6 foot or 4 foot) leash.

Role of Obedience Training

With separation anxious dogs, we want to encourage them to attach and bond to other things and animals in their environment. This can occur if we let them sniff and move about freely to become absorbed with the scents and sights out there. Some humans have dogs with serious separation issues that threaten their very survival and yet they insist their dogs heel when they go for walks in the park. Heeling doesn't come naturally to dogs and we might speculate it's not nearly as enjoyable as sniffing around. In addition, the dog has to focus intently on the owner to stay at heel. Get the picture? On-leash, we should not insist they tune into us unless absolutely necessary to meet another critical behavioral goal. For example, it doesn't help any dog if we let them bark and lunge at passing dogs; we would have to divert them from this aggressive activity.

If your dog's anxiety is triggered when you leave a room, another strategy some behaviorists recommend is to teach him to lie down and stay. When the dog is able to stay in place, you can increase your distance until you are out of the room. At first, return quickly (in 30 seconds) and then leave for longer periods. As an alternative, when your dog is hungry, you can scatter a mix of treats and dog food all over the floor and walk out of the room. If Super-Motivating treats are part of the mix your dog will likely grow to enjoy your departures—if you go slowly and gradually lengthen the time you are away.

Another Dog for Companionship?

Families searching for solutions will ask, "What if we got a second dog to keep (our dog) company all day?" Unfortunately, most (though not all) of the separation anxious dogs I've worked with were not comforted by having other dogs in the home. The humans were central, not other dogs.

When to Rehome?

If families must be away all day, rehoming can be one of the better options, if a suitable home can be found. It's important that we understand what's going on with the dog, what the symptoms are, how they are tied in with the relationship with humans and other animals in the home. Does the dog remain upset all day, or just as you are leaving, or any time there is a physical separation? When we plan interventions, as always they have to be orchestrated to fit the dog.

Another question that matters: Are other pets in the home, such as dogs and cats, stressed by the separation anxious dog's frantic expression of their misery? Cassie's human, Janet, set up a camera to videotape her dogs while she was out of the house, and the Greyhound slept and ate and played and didn't seem bothered by Cassie, so we didn't have to worry that the Greyhound would be harmed as we struggled to help Cassie.

Too many families feel defeated when their dogs have to be rehomed, or alternatively, seek to punish errant dogs by banishing them. I wish they were more concerned with getting at-risk dogs with reasonably good prognoses to safe harbors. I recently encountered a Toy dog with a difficult past who was inappropriately placed in a home with early elementary-aged children. This was a mistake. He bonded beautifully with the mother but didn't want to have to share her with children. He growled and lunged, though never actually bit them. The mother felt protective of her children and wanted the dog gone immediately. She impugned the "character" of a dog who would bite children, i.e. he must be "a bad dog" and she wanted her family rid of him, fast.

Harkening back to my discussion in the first section about the Bichon who was hit by a car, we might view the mother's approach to protecting her children from harm as short-sighted. There are more valuable lessons the children could have learned from their experience with the anxious seven pounder: their family's values and love remain strong in the face of life's challenges; some creatures (humans included) not suited to one set of circumstances might perform beautifully in other settings; we have an ethical obligation to give them safe passage, if we can. Dogs can be contained so they don't have opportunities to harm while we search for alternative arrangements.

> *"Although the idea that an animal will stay forever in one home is lovely...there are many good reasons for animals to be rehomed...and we should rejoice in the fact that most animals adjust well and learn to love again. The critical question is not whether the animal was rehomed, but whether he was moved from his previous home responsibly."*
>
> Sheila Webster Boneham, PhD, *Rescue Matters*

Shayna Goes to Church

> *"That would be a very Christian thing
> for our parishioners to do!"*

Caregivers who are committed to helping their dogs can be quite inventive. Niki Lamproplos, an experienced dog behavior consultant (master's of arts degree in psychology) in private practice in Greensburg, Pennsylvania, told me this story about a sweet Labrador retriever, Shayna, who couldn't tolerate being home alone, and her humans who were determined to help her.

It should come as no surprise that a dog like Shayna has issues with separation. In her short life, she had experienced the callousness people can exhibit toward animals. Stuffed in a small cage, she was bred every time she came into season, to produce puppies for the financial gain of an owner who cared about her solely for commercial purposes. In other words, he made money selling her puppies.

Shayna was eventually "rescued" from her constricted life by a woman who collected dogs and decided to breed her yet again. Her ersatz rescuer later wanted to "get rid of" some dogs. She tried to sell Shayna at a flea market, but with no buyers in sight, Shayna laid her head on the woman's leg and looked up at her with liquid hazel eyes; the woman grumbled that she guessed she would have to take her home again.

It so happened that, at about the same time, a pastor and his wife, Wes and Bunny, had lost their beloved Labrador to old age and were looking for a new dog. They wanted to adopt one that needed rescuing. Friends told them about the woman who owned Shayna and was trying to place her, so they took the long trip to visit her. From the moment Shayna met Wes, she was attached and tried to always be at his side.

Wes and Bunny led a quiet life, and much of their free time was now focused on Shayna. They felt the adoption was meant to be. She fit into their lives almost seamlessly…as long as she could be with them! Sundays put a crinkle in their plans for Shayna. Wes was the pastor of a church and couldn't help but notice that Shayna became agitated when the couple prepared to leave for services. She followed them from room to room with a worried look. When they returned they would find small things chewed up.

Wes suspected Shayna suffered from separation distress. For affirmation, one Sunday the couple pulled their car out of the garage and waited just outside the door, where they heard the heartbreaking sound of Shayna howling. On Monday they discussed the problem with their veterinarian who referred them to Niki.

It's difficult to help dogs like Shayna because they are at their worst when the people who love them aren't there to comfort and guide them. Each family's resources are different. Few families can have someone stay at home with a worried dog around the clock. Shayna was to find happiness, however, because of the grace, compassion and competence of team Wes and Bunny, the two dedicated professionals: Niki and the referring veterinarian, and parishioners who understood what it meant to be followers of Christ.

Wes and Bunny were semi-retired so their schedules were flexible and could be adapted to Shayna's need. Niki developed a behavior modification plan that called for Shayna to not be left alone during the retraining period, for approximately 6 weeks. Their only sticking point was when both Wes and Bunny had to leave the house together for church on Sundays. They explored the possibility of having neighbors or friends sit with Shayna during these times, but none were available. Niki lightheartedly suggested that perhaps Shayna should go to church with them for the next few months. Wes's face lit up and he commented, "That would be a very Christian thing for our parishioners to do!"

Indeed, it would!

Over the next few days Bunny called each member of their church, explained the situation, and asked if they would agree to have Shayna attend services for a few months. So began Shayna's church membership. Each Sunday she accompanied the couple to church. They brought along a mat and some toys for her and she sat with Bunny in the pew while Wes led the service. As she became comfortable in her new environment, Shayna began greeting the parishioners and became a real part of their church.

The program to help Shayna stay home alone comfortably was successful and the time came when Wes and Bunny could leave her for five or six hours and return to find her curled up on the couch sleeping. She no longer needed church. However, as Wes and Bunny discovered, the church members needed her! And so it is, Shayna still attends services each Sunday, and she's included in special holiday meals and activities at the church. Her sweet spirit graces the parish that opened their hearts to her in her time of need. A delightful reciprocity unfolded and Shayna found her calling.

Murphy's Choice

Murphy was a fourteen months old, thirty pound, neutered Beagle mix who was "the sweetest dog ever" when he was not snarling and lunging at people. He was adopted at the age of ten months by a couple, Cheryl and Bob, whose children were grown and out of the house. They were referred to me by Murphy's veterinarian.

I ask prospective clients to complete a lengthy behavior questionnaire that I review before scheduling to meet with them. Looking over Murphy's information, I knew Cheryl and Bob would welcome me in to their home, but Murphy would not. In fact, if I didn't manage the situation well, he would bite me.

Dogs that Bite

In our society, dogs that bite are at high risk of losing their homes and their lives. It can be difficult to impossible, and sometimes not entirely ethical, to rehome them. Many rescue groups don't take in dogs with bite histories, sometimes regardless of the circumstances of the bite. Keep in mind, however, a few rescuers have the mind-set to save every dog and will rehome dogs known to be aggressive, to unsuspecting adopters. Similarly, many relinquishing families neglect to mention their dogs have issues and some aggression does not surface in animal shelters before dogs are placed.

Families are typically pressured by extended family, neighbors, and friends to "get rid of" their aggressive dogs. These dogs can seem like pariahs in a litigious society where dogs that bite are a threat to family's financial security. (See the Dog Bite Law Web site, www.dogbitelaw.com, for information on the legal and economic ramifications in the various states.)

In addition, I have clients who believe any dog that bites should be euthanized, partially because that's what their parents and grandparents believed before them. These clients might pretend their dogs didn't actually bite anyone, in spite of evidence to the contrary (including blood), so they can be faithful to their family's beliefs and yet let their dogs live on. If they persist in believing all dogs that bite humans should be euthanized, I of course do not try to get them to face the reality that their dog did indeed bite...if the behavior can be modified without their admitting to the facts.

In spite of all the doom and gloom surrounding aggression, I regularly encounter families who will hang in there for their dogs in need, even if the problem is aggression. Some have compassionate relatives and neighbors who similarly ask, "What can we do?" In my experience, a lot of aggressive behavior can be modified fairly quickly, and if there's a reasonable chance of success, why not try?

The caveat to this is that I do meet dogs with real potential to harm and if they can't be made trustworthy, we must be realistic and cognizant of our responsibilities to protect others, including the dogs and cats that cross their path.

Don't Trigger Aggression

My first responsibility during a consult, to the dogs and the families that love them, is to not trigger an aggressive display or a bite. As such, I try to keep dogs below threshold. There's no time like the present for modifying dog behavior. My charge is to figure out how to get the behavior to not happen.

Dogs typically use growling and biting to drive people away. If they succeed, they employ these methods again to accomplish similar ends. Behavior that is reinforced quickly becomes habit. As such, I do whatever I can to keep dogs at the level of grumble warnings, so they don't escalate to the point where they are "gone" and out of control, because then it's too late to modify their behavior. (As a reminder to readers, a threshold is "the point at which a stimulus is of sufficient intensity to begin to produce an effect."[83])

I similarly want families to protect their dogs from triggers and keep them below threshold, from the time of the consult forward. They must provide their dogs with opportunities to practice their new, more adaptive behaviors.

Murphy's Adaptation to his Family

Cheryl and Bob are experienced dog owners. Cheryl works from an office in the home and Bob works outside the home. All we know about Murphy's origins is that he was a Hurricane Katrina survivor. He was playful at the shelter and licked Cheryl's hand and, "with those big brown eyes and sweet face, he asked me to take him home."

Murphy quickly bonded with Cheryl and was not unfriendly to Bob. He was not completely housetrained but Cheryl went back to the basics and had him eliminating reliably in a preferred location outside within three weeks.

Additional problems surfaced in those weeks, however...

Dog's carry-over problems typically become manifest within their first three weeks in a new home. When dogs don't show some misbehavior initially,

---

83   *Random House Dictionary*, s.v. threshold <http://www.dictionary.com>.

adoptive families are apt to blame themselves when it surfaces weeks later, though it's really a matter of dogs growing comfortable and bonded enough to show us their full orientation.

As an aside, I worked with several female dogs with no prior reported history of aggression, but they were aggressive towards humans in their new homes. The families wonder, why didn't the shelters tell them about the aggression? A common factor was the dogs were spayed immediately before placement with their new families. There's no research that I know of to support this, but I've wondered if the surgery with anesthesia, medications and pain, coupled with the adjustment to a new setting, stimulates aggression in a small percentage of dogs. The shelters usually have limited funds and can't afford to alter dogs that might not be adopted, so they have a compelling reason to wait until the days before an adoption to do this surgery on their dogs. I wish they could focus instead on easing female dog's transitions to new homes. Some owners return these "aggressive" dogs to the shelters; among the owners who hung in there and bonded with them, the aggression fully dissipated within weeks after the surgery and rehoming.

Aggression to Visitors

After a few weeks in his new home, Murphy started growling ferociously at visitors to the house. He bit a delivery man who walked in his yard, on the back of his leg. It was what we call an "inhibited" bite that barely broke skin and the delivery man didn't make an issue of it. Murphy could have done damage but he did not.

Murphy growls and snaps at the couple's adult daughter when she visits and nips at her heels. The daughter reportedly has a loud voice, rushes through the house, insists on trying to pet Murphy, and when he tenses up and growls, she shrinks back fearfully. We might speculate this sequence both frightens and emboldens him. The house and yard had become "his" territory. I assessed there was a fear component to the territorial aggression.

Leash Aggression

Similarly, When Cheryl took Murphy on walks, he growled and lunged at passers-by, human and dog, and gave chase to loud moving vehicles such as buses and motorcycles.

DNA Testing for Mixed Breeds

With the nipping at heels and chasing I thought he was a Beagle mixed with one of the herding breeds such as Australian Cattle Dogs. Families who want to know the genetically determined breed composition of their dogs can have them tested. Some tests can be administered at home; you would send in the swab results. Others require a blood sample and are done in a veterinarian's office. Your veterinarian might be a good source of information on genetic testing that yields reliable results.

Dog Trainer's Input

Cheryl and Bob hoped obedience training would help and they signed Murphy up for classes. He quickly learned to sit, lie down, stay and walk at heel by Cheryl's side. He did a lovely heel but broke ranks when he caught sight of people, animals and moving vehicles outside the training center.

Cheryl explained his ongoing problems to the trainer and the trainer introduced her to a remote controlled, electronic collar and advised her to "stimulate", or shock Murphy, when he growled or lunged. Murphy responded to the punishment from the electronic collar by escalating from low rumbles to deep growling and curled lips. His problems were getting worse!

Warning Growls are Good

As a point of information, dogs growl to warn us of what's to come if we persist at what we're doing that bothers them. It's not in our interests to punish dogs for growling. Dogs that have giving up on growling as a defense may escalate to biting, without the warning.

Punishment Again

In addition, punishment with a shock collar might cow an aggressive dog to submission but it doesn't make the dog feel better about the things that upset him and it doesn't change the triggers. It doesn't give him information about what he should be doing. This quote by Abraham Lincoln hits the target of the issue: "Force is all-conquering, but its victories are short-lived.[84] I have not yet met an aggressive dog that could be punished out of his aggression (though some trainers claim otherwise), but most dogs I work with can be lured away from aggression to more acceptable behaviors.

Most Indispensible Tool

Murphy survived Katrina but could he survive his own dark impulses? The veterinarian, family and I were pulling for him. Desperate times call for drastic measures, as the saying goes. I asked Cheryl to have Murphy on a leash

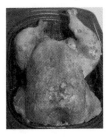

when I arrived. In addition, I brought along with me the most effective, anti-unprovoked aggression combat tool ever. On my way to the consult I stopped by Sam's Club to pick up an aromatic Fresh-Roasted Rotisserie Chicken!

At this point you might think, "Good grief, Hoover's going to bribe the dog!" This is not true; I don't ever pursue mistrustful, scared dogs with food because I don't want them feeling (in dog emotional language) "I thought she was scary and she is, though her chicken sure is tasty."

When I walked in to the house with my chicken I didn't look at Murphy or try to interact with him in any way. He growled and air sniffed and finally lay down about ten feet away from me. He snarled viciously, with lips curled up. That boy had me dead in his sights. His growling was interspersed with air sniffing. We were all getting hungry, but Murphy was still snarling at me.

Confinement and Use of Distance

During a consult, I want to see what happens when families move their aggressive dogs to an out-of-the-way spot in the house, for example, to a bedroom or basement with the doors closed, or a crate at a distance and out

....
84   Julia B. Hoitt, *Excellent Quotations for Home and School* (1888). 97.

of view of their families. As such, I asked Cheryl to move Murphy from the kitchen to an adjoining room. He went willingly. She gave him a chew toy and closed the door. We didn't hear another peep from him while we plotted his future. I asked Cheryl to check in on him periodically; he was quiet, relaxed, chewing his toy, and not interested in us.

Some aggressive dogs have to be part of the action and will bark and intensify their complaint when their families put them out of sight. Our goal is to reduce an aggressive dog's reactivity and arousal; as such, we can't use enforced distancing with these dogs. Similarly, when we confine some aggressive dogs to crates, they go wild. This arousal increases the likelihood they will bite when released. With these dogs, we again can't use confinement or removal to a distance because these particular strategies would escalate things.

Many dogs are like Murphy and being placed at a distance from "triggers" such as visitors like me has an immediate calming effect on them. Dogs calmed in this way are a whole lot easier to work with because families have a sure-fire, easy way to avoid triggering the aggression when they have company.

We had a winner with the room! As such, we agreed that in the future Murphy wouldn't be allowed to "greet" visitors unless Cheryl was there and could carry out behavior protocols, or until Murphy could be friendly towards people entering the house. Cheryl would end the visitor drama by simply putting him in another room, giving him a chew toy, and closing the door. If there was a danger that visitors such as children would open the door, she would have to put a lock it.

As indicated, if Murphy had protested his "banishment", we couldn't have used out-of-sight confinement as a strategy in our behavior management plan.

Murphy's Allowed Out of the Room

After fifteen minutes I asked Cheryl to bring Murphy out of the room. Interestingly, he was like a different dog with me. The tension was gone; I told Cheryl she could unfasten his leash. Murphy headed right for me and stood there looking longingly at my chicken. He sat when I asked him to sit and I gave him a few pieces of chicken. He kept offering behaviors, trying to figure out how he could get me to give him more of the scrumptious Rotisserie Chicken. After this I could work easily with him.

Murphy was relaxed and so was I. I had taken the lid off the chicken and he adored me…okay, maybe it was the chicken he loved. Whatever, he was now treating me as a benefactor, not a stranger. When I saw how easy it was for him to interact with me, after we bypassed the drama that occurs every time visitors arrive, I knew he would be okay. He needed some work, it would take several months to shake off old habits and create new ones, but he was going to be okay.

We now had Murphy making the right choices about a visitor. This is what we want from aggressive dogs. My Rotisserie Chicken helped change his mind about the role of visitors in his life. Whereas he had been threatening, now he was a delightful mooch with tail waving happily in the air.

It's not about giving aggressive, menacing dogs fresh-roasted chicken— though I haven't found a dog who would admit to that. It's about having something good on me but not trying to woo him with it. Instead, I wait until I can see what structural arrangements are necessary for the dog to accept the chicken with me as part of the package. Through experimentation, we discovered that if Murphy was put in another room for a short time, he'd come out relaxed and hungry. Greetings triggered aggression so why not just skip greetings for a while?

Families can feel overwhelmed and not realize their dog's aggression is not as widespread as it appears. Observation shows us what triggers aggression and what elicits calm, soft responses.

Owner Compliance

Murphy had another thing going for him: his special person, Cheryl, was good with dogs and enthusiastic about carrying out our behavior plans. Noncompliance is dangerous for dogs and people. I tend to get the best compliance from humans whose dogs are like "children", next from families whose children are launched, and the least compliance from families with preschoolers.

Visitors to Ignore Murphy

Going forward, Cheryl agreed to ask visitors, including her daughter, to ignore Murphy when they come to the house. This is an example of a structural change humans can make to help dogs lose their "bad" habits and replace them with new, human-preferred patterns. Cheryl told her daughter if she couldn't walk quietly through the house and ignore Murphy, she was not to visit. This might sound harsh but we were on a roll! We knew we could help Murphy.

Super-Motivating Treats

I recommended that Cheryl engage Murphy in the process of making Super-Motivating treats (see instructions in the "Behavior Cache" section). Cheryl would squeak the toy, call "Chickie!" and deliver a treat. This was not to be used for obedience training but to get a conditioned response from Murphy, who would quickly become more interested in the treats than his "triggers" and would prefer getting treats over feeling stressed by visitors and having his special person, Cheryl, upset with him.

I also showed Cheryl how to get his attention using a squeaky toy followed by a Super-Motivating treat or other reward. Cheryl was to divert his attention away from visitors to the house, to the reinforcers. I was confident the toy and treats would soon interest him more than the visitors.

As a reminder, Murphy's trigger was visitors to the home. If he met up with people already in the home, he was not as bothered or likely to react, especially if the visitors appeared more friend that foe by bringing gifts of food.

Relaxation Strategies

Anything that increased Murphy's relaxation would be a plus. Cheryl and Bob wanted to try all of the strategies available to them. When they had visitors, they played harp music to relax Murphy. They used a Comfort Zone dog appeasing pheromone plug-in purchased from their veterinarian.[85] They created an anxiety wrap using a T-shirt with Velcro, bought at Walmart for a

85   Farnam Comfort Zone Plug-In Diffuser with Feliway, <http://www.amazon.com>.

few dollars and invested in a video that showed them how to use TTouch to help Murphy relax.[86]

Specifically, Cheryl would bring out all the relaxers when they were expecting visitors and employ them during the time visitors were in the house.

Leash Aggression

Next we had to tackle the problem with leash aggression. We fitted Murphy with a front-clip (SENSE-ation) harness. I usually get a rough fit and let the owner make it tighter. However, Murphy actually allowed me to adjust his harness! This was the dog that had been frightening and menacing a half hour earlier. The tricky part is that interventions can rarely be applied to individual dogs in the same way to yield positive results. We have to fish around and listen to feedback from our dogs to know how to draw winning responses. My questions are always, how do we get the behavior we don't want to not happen, and how do we get the behavior we do want to happen more often?

We took Murphy outside, with pieces from the chicken in a small, plastic bag and a Kong slathered with peanut butter. He put his nose down to sniff and explore. He was so busy he didn't see a dog with her person in the distance and he just glanced at a car passing by, whereas previously he would have been combative and drawn to chase. He didn't pay attention to the others, that is, until Cheryl pulled him away from his sniffing and commanded him to "Heel!" I asked, "What the heck are you doing?" She said he is supposed to walk by her side like she taught him to do in obedience classes. Murphy quickly showed us both the shortcomings of her strategy: he tuned in to a person walking a dog and growled and lunged at them. Good grief! Cheryl could help Murphy outside, in two ways:

Murphy should be free to do what's natural for him, sniffing and exploring. He seemed to prefer this activity to getting all upset and going after passers-by. He let us know by his behavior that exploration was enjoyable.

---

86   Tellington Touch Videos for dogs, <http://www.ttouch.com>.

The harness thwarted Murphy so it was not as comfortable when he barked and lunged. In addition, Cheryl squeaked the toy and used chicken, the Kong and other treats to lure Murphy away from his "triggers". She positively re-inforced him for letting go of his interest in "triggers", or for "opting out" and redirecting his interests to the rewards. He responded immediately and favorably to these interventions.

In the "Behavior Cache" section, "Dog to Dog Approaches", you will find descriptions of three approaches to dealing with leash aggression. The ap-proach I most often employ is to give dogs the alternatives to opt out or let go of their interest in their triggers instead of dramatizing their discomfort and feeling horrible about it, as we would feel if we became all stressed out and lost our cool during encounters with our triggers.

Progress Report

Cheryl worked hard and stayed with the behavior modification and manage-ment plan. Within two months she could take Murphy anywhere, including dog parks, and he didn't accost anyone or fight with dogs. Visitors arrived, inside and outside, and he sniffed around instead of growling, snarling and threatening.

Why was Murphy so adaptable? He sounded really vicious at the outset, but I suppose he essentially liked people and dogs and appears to have had posi-tive experiences with them in the past. He's part Beagle and Beagles like to eat and sniff and follow trails and eat again. He got to sniff and eat, eat and sniff, and these diversions apparently were satisfying and fun enough replace-ments and they quickly trumped his interest in being as offensive as possible towards visitors. His great relationship with Cheryl and good-enough rela-tionship with Bob surely helped.

The Best Offense

Cadet is a composite of three dogs with similar problems associated with their breed; before contacting me through referrals from their veterinarians, all three families had used remote electronic collars on their dogs with similar, negative results. My reason for going with a composite is to protect reputations.

Cadet is a sixteen-month-old Anatolian shepherd with a picture-perfect life—or so it would seem. He has what America's crate-captive dogs must yearn for: the freedom to move around without restraint. He lives with a family that loves him, with two outdoor acres completely surrounded by see-through fencing secure enough to keep pets in and wildlife out. A gate across the driveway blocks unwelcome entries from strangers. However, at the time of the consult, Cadet was the real force that prevented strangers and friends from planting their boots on the ground there.

Cadet moved in with his family at the age of eight weeks, fresh out of his litter. By eight months he was a rowdy adolescent with the freedom to roam throughout the acreage, with minimal supervision.

Cadet spent several hours a day alone in the yard, doing whatever he wanted, while his family went about their lives. He was always welcome inside, and he liked to hang out with his family, but he enjoyed a lot of outdoor freedom.

Cadet's problems became serious after an incident that occurred when he was twelve months old. The gate was left open during a snowstorm and a stranded stranger wandered up the driveway looking for assistance. Cadet barked and growled ferociously and the man retreated to his car. Whereas

Cadet previously traveled the fence line in a somewhat haphazard fashion, from this time forward he prowled up and down, looking for anything that didn't seem quite right to him.

Unfortunately, Cadet didn't have the ability to distinguish between friend and foe, so almost anyone on the outside was lumped as "stranger" and when he caught sight of a stranger, he would growl deeply and rush the fence. His family tried to call him off but he ignored them. From the looks of it, he found a job that matched his abilities and he did not intend to give it up.

Visitors couldn't enter the grounds unless the family physically removed Cadet. Friends stopped visiting because they were afraid of him. The neighbors on one side could not walk about their property adjacent to Cadet's "side" of the fence, without being threatened. The wise dog-neighbors on the other side did not have a problem with him. They spared themselves by befriending Cadet when he was a puppy and, with his family's permission, brought him beef marrow bones from the supermarket and invited him over to play often enough to be included on Cadet's very short list of extra-familial "friends".

Cadet was stirring things up elsewhere. He growled and lunged at the insurance salesman who couldn't then recommend the family for a homeowner's policy, and the Fed-Ex delivery man refused to come further than the gate, even after he was assured by the family that Cadet would be confined to the house on days they expected deliveries. Trying to avoid another incident, Cadet's family took to tracking deliveries on the Internet. They posted "Beware of Dog" signs and hoped for the best.

Occasionally strangers would come to the door when Cadet was in the house with his family. He would react with fierce growling and barking and would not lie down until the stranger passed out of view or entered the house. Once visitors were in the house and sitting down, however, he quickly warmed to them, though in the past weeks he started tensing up when they got out of their seats to move about the house.

Other than this, Cadet was lovely with his family though he did present himself for petting (on-demand), barked when he wanted food, and put himself in the middle of things. All family members agreed, "He likes to be the center of attention!"

Trainer's Input

When Cadet was eleven weeks old his family started taking him to classes for training. He learned his basic commands—sit, lie down, wait, stay, come here, and leave it—and enjoyed playing with the other puppies and their humans. The problem now was Cadet would not come when called if he was "on patrol". With the incident at twelve months and the ratcheting up of guarding behavior, his family decided to take him back for more training.

The trainer had twenty years of experience with dogs in classes and said he specialized in aggression. He diagnosed Cadet as having "territorial and dominance aggression" and told the family they had to "get tough" with him. He observed it would not be possible for family members to get compliance from Cadet as long he was free to run the fence line at a distance.

Electronic Collar

To counteract this problem of having no control over Cadet when he was loose in the yard, the trainer told them to buy a remote training collar with a range that would cover the full acreage. He would show them how to use it.

They bought the recommended electronic collar with five adjustable levels of stimulation. They could now let Cadet run around in the yard, call him to "Come here!" and when he didn't obey they applied a stimulation, or shock to his neck. The goal was to teach Cadet he must come on command, no matter what.

The family was initially pleased with the results. Cadet came when called, every time. His behavior was impeccable for at least three weeks. One friend was so impressed he signed his own dog up for training at the same center.

However, all was not as well as it seemed with Cadet. After the few "good" weeks, he went back to patrolling, but with greater ferocity. The family dutifully used the remote but he seemed oblivious to the shocks to his neck. One day, the mother was just outside the gate, welcoming a friend, and Cadet hurled himself at the gate. The friend was too frightened to continue her visit and fled for the safety of her car.

Cadet had simply stopped responding to the shocks. The family feared more than ever that their otherwise gentle dog, weighing 100 pounds, was going to hurt someone. Their veterinarian referred them to me.

My Assessment

What are we to think about Cadet? He certainly fits the stereotype for territorial aggression, but is the trainer's assessment of dominance aggression justified? I think not, though it appears Cadet was a confident and assertive dog whose relationship with his humans could use some adjustment that would render him more deferential to his humans and their leadership. Cadet's problem was he assumed executive powers when, unbeknownst to him, he did not have the judgment to be entrusted with executive responsibilities; in short, he could not tell the difference between predators and strollers. Big problem. His patrolling must have been self-reinforcing—we can be sure that when a behavior is not in some ways satisfying, or reinforcing, dogs don't repeat it.

The prime issue here is Cadet's breed. What do we humans think Anatolian shepherds are apt to do, unsupervised and alone, with time on their hands? We can find the answer to that question by doing a Google.com search for Anatolians on the Internet, and or by referencing reputable breed books.

Anatolian Shepherds

" …Very loyal, alert…possessive with respect to their home and property and will not allow anyone into the family property if the owner is not home, unless (they have had) frequent contact with the persons… but (they are) fairly friendly with those people the family accepts… very loyal, alert…suspicious of strangers, especially after reaching adulthood. Strangers should be formally introduced before the mature dogs are asked to accept them…They already have very strong protection instincts that grow as they mature…"[87]

Most dogs engage in some territorial aggression, even highly sociable, ever-friendly breeds such as the Bichon Frise. Labrador retrievers can be fiercer guard dogs than they are given credit for, probably due to the perception and fact that they can be won over with steak or even plain dog biscuits. Anatolians and other guarding breeds, on the other hand, are more serious about guarding and they stake out defined territories. Fence lines help them establish boundaries between "ours" and "not ours". German shepherds, Dobermans, Rottweilers, Bull-Mastiffs, American bulldogs, Belgian shepherds, and some of the terriers are examples of breeds that are apt to be more intense about establishing and guarding territories.

At this point at least one of you is probably saying, "But we had a shepherd growing up and he was a big baby who just wanted belly rubs!!" It's true; many dogs are not true to type. Whatever the exceptions, Cadet showed territorial aggression that is normal for a dog of his breed that had freedom to roam from a young age. He was a guard dog. What were we to expect him to do—not guard?

Living with Guarding Breeds

Cadet's family could have curbed his territorial, guarding tendencies early on if they had carefully supervised his outdoor activities from puppyhood through adolescence. By the time he reached adulthood he would have different yard habits that did not include rushing the fence line. They could have kept him on a lead much of the time and provided entertainment, excite-

87 Dog Breed Information. Anatolian Shepherds, <http:www.dogbreedinfo.com/anatolianshepherd.htm>.

ment, and distractions towards the center of the yard and away from the perimeters. Using food as a reinforcer, the family could have asked the neighbors on all sides to toss Cadet beef marrow bones when he was young and invite him to their yards to visit, to prevent problems later.

It appears the remote collar helped briefly and then exacerbated Cadet's aggression. His guard-dog habits were now deeply ingrained, and if left to run, his aggression would likely intensify with age, and would be passed along in full force when he transitioned from adolescence to adulthood.

In the days of big farms and homesteads, Cadet would have been appreciated as one of his family's most valuable assets, capable as he was of keeping humans and livestock safe from predators. In our current age, however, if Cadet were to bite a passer-by he could be declared a dangerous dog and the situation would deteriorate for him from there—the negative fallout for being his natural self and doing a job he takes seriously. His behavior was putting him at-risk of losing everything.

The family might have prevented problems if they had put a solid fence around the property, not see-through. If you have or plan to get a dog that responds to visuals such as people and dogs walking past your property and you are looking at fence styles, go with a solid fence and create interesting activity to the center of the yard, away from the fence line. I wish I were in a position to advise more families with difficult to raise dogs about how to elicit the best lifetime behaviors from their dogs, from the outset. We could prevent so many problems that obedience training alone will not circumvent.

Problem-Solving

What are we to do for guard dogs after they have discovered the joys of patrolling? Whatever we provide in its stead has to also be pleasurable and pleasurable enough to counteract other interests. As with other behavior problems, we have to prevent the behavior we don't want from happening and provide distractions and diversions to help dogs establish new habits that will not put them in such direct conflict with their environment.

First and foremost, we must not try to force dogs like Cadet out of behavior that is genetically inspired. Remember, dogs can be lured and wooed. As such, I recommended the family take him outside on a long flexi-lead or alternatively a long line such as the thirty footers used to lunge thousand pound horses—they are surely strong enough to contain hundred pound dogs. The family agreed to limit his freedom for months, maybe even a whole year, and trips outside would include different types of fun. For example, they could engage him in ball play, hide-and-seek, and other games. They created a dig box in a landscaped area at a distance from the fence lines, and hid bones and toys in the area. All around the yard, they dropped treats and chew toys so he had something interesting to do when he was in the yard. (See suggestions in the "Behavior Cache" section for providing a "Stimulating Environment" for dogs that need action, and "Digging and Lawn Problems".) On hot summer days he could cool off and "fish" for ice cubes and toys in a small swimming pool set up just for him.

Meanwhile, Cadet needed a better recall; the best time to teach a recall is when the dog is on the other end of a leash or long line. Cadet improved at coming when called, fast, after his family conditioned him to respond enthusiastically to the promise of "Chickies", (the Super-Motivating treats explained in the "Behavior Cache" section.) "Chickies" are so positively reinforcing that Cadet was soon letting go of his interest in what was going on at the fence line and redirecting his interest to the "Chickies". He could not help himself, fickle dog. "Chickies" taste good and it must have been fun for him to try to figure out how to get his humans to give him some.

One key to using food treats successfully is to fade them out as dogs develop new, people-preferred habits.

Over the months, Cadet gradually lost interest in the parameters and he developed a lasting interest in what was going on inside the fence. After a few months they could let him off the long line or flexi-leash, but would stay out there with him. After six months they could let him outside by himself, to eliminate in the yard. If they left him for too long, he would wander over to the fence and they knew they had to put him back on a line. He was always a bit edgy at the parameters and the family would have to keep up vigilance for the rest of his life, though over time he grew able to handle more freedoms.

I wish we could have given Cadet something "legal" to guard but there was not a real job for him in the family, except for mild guarding in the house at night. He would travel from bedroom to bedroom to make sure his family was safe. Intruders would be sorry if they invaded his house.

Establishing Leadership

There's a protocol behaviorists and trainers have been using for years, called "Nothing in Life is Free".[88] It helps humans establish leadership. The idea is to not give your dog resources, or positive reinforcers, until the dog has done something that is asked of him. When a dog like Cadet presents himself for petting, his humans might ask him to sit and lie down and sit again, and if he doesn't do as they ask he doesn't get the rewards (positive reinforcers). Remember, all we need from our dogs is simple deference. Just ask our dogs to sit and when they sit, we've "won" the lead.

The exception is the dog that is overly "operant", meaning the dog has us too well-trained to ask for a sit so he can sit and get the reward. In that case, the dog might be in the lead, not us. We can shake things up by asking the dog to do something that doesn't bring a reward, and he does it just to get us off his back. Whatever it takes, I know I have the lead as soon as a dog relaxes, moves along when I ask him to, and looks at me expectantly. It's all very subtle. With some in-charge dogs I might use a drill sergeant, tough-trainer-type voice: "SIT!" It makes me laugh when I use myself in a purposeful way like this. Stern but playful: "SIT!" "LIE DOWN!" Devout dog-friendly trainers are ostensibly supposed to not use such techniques, but an occasional dog loves Sergeant Hoover; my language puts them in a relationship with me that I'm certain they absolutely enjoy, especially if their families have been overly nurturing with them. Nurturance is wonderful, and I deeply appreciate nurturing families, but too much of a good thing locks some problems in place.

Dominance Language

At this point, I encourage you to peruse the literature on dominance termi-

---

88 Nothing in Life is Free protocols are on the Internet. See <http://www.k9deb.com/nilif.htm> by Deb McKean, and <http://www.ddfl.org/behavior/nilif.pdf> by the Dumb Friends League.

nology. (See "Dominance" in the "Behavior Cache" section). If you're inclined to attach the "dominance" label to your dogs, read the dominance articles listed and e-mail me at dogquirks@gmail.com to let me know what you think. The articles might help you understand why dominance thinking so often gets in the way of problem-solving.

Resource Guarding

My Yorkshire terrier, Piper, guards precious resources such as his toy Buster Cube and me. He will lie next to his Buster Cube for hours, as if every passing person and dog wants it as much as he does. We call this behavior "resource guarding" or in medical model terms "possessive aggression." We manage it by limiting his access to the Buster Cubes, except on his birthday or a few cold winter days when we can't get out for walks! When we give him chewies, we put him in a room alone so he won't growl at our Labrador, Andy. We use indirect methods to take objects he values from him, such as luring him with a high-value treat or snatching a treasured item quickly followed up by petting him in a loving way that conveys acceptance for his whole self. As such, we avoid getting into direct conflict with him. If he guards space, he loses the space. For example, when he guards his spot up high on the bed, we put him on the floor for half a minute; when he returns he's more relaxed and deferential. Some families "punish" their dogs for their transgressions by depriving them of resources for hours or their whole lives, but why do this if its not accomplishing anything? If the dog is deferential after a few seconds, why bother with hours or forever? Human teenagers might need days to consider what they've done, but dogs tend to realize instantly. If their aggression causes them to lose precious resources, and deference gets them back, they will likely choose deference to get the resources. Similarly, if aggression wins them resources, of course aggression will become the modus operandi.

Resource guarding is different than territorial aggression. Resource guarders are possessive. Dogs like Cadet guard against perceived predators that, as they see it, might bring harm to them and their families.

Dog-to-Dog Household Aggression

I've received many calls from families with more than one dog and they are frantic because the dogs are fighting. This can manifest as horrible, loud skirmishes where no one is injured, or at the extreme to fights that result in injuries requiring medical treatment.

Fighting can occur due to "personality clashes", for example, when one dog is too intense or intrusive for the other dog. The most important first intervention is to separate the dogs to prevent another occurrence. If every dog owner followed this advice to immediately separate their fighting dogs, far more dog-to-dog household aggression would be resolved. At a certain point, after a number of skirmishes, the distrust between the dogs is so deep and beyond repair that the best option might be to rehome one dog—if a home can be found. However, in cases where one dog overwhelms the other dog, I've had tremendous success using the strategy described below.

Reinforce Dogs for Letting Go of Interest in Other Dog and Tuning Them Out

Management. When two dogs in a household are fighting, I might ask their families to keep both dogs on leads, to manage their movements in the house and yard to prevent aggressive displays or fighting. The less fights, the better their chances of success. My goal is to have zero fights from the time of my consult onward.

Super-Motivating Treats as Reinforcers. It is virtually impossible to condition two dogs to the Super-Motivating treats at the same time, if they are already fighting. You have to work with dogs individually for a while because excitement over the treats can provoke more aggression. (The protocol for conditioning dogs to respond automatically to these reinforcers is in the "Behavior Cache" section of the book. All protocols have to be tweaked a bit according to the response patterns of individual dogs. This is where a competent behaviorist would be helpful because they have the ability to pick up on minute cues.)

Once a dog can be 'swept up' by the Super-Motivating treats, you can use them to consistently divert one dog's attention away from the other dog and reward both dogs for turning their heads away. Reinforce even the slightest turns away from the other dog. Any turn-away is an improvement.

Teach Both Dogs to Tune Out. Each dog needs a family member that is committed to teaching him to always turn away from and let go of any interest in the dog they previously fought with. You are building up to something that you want to hold for the lifetime of the two dogs living under the same roof. It is especially important to accomplish "tuning out" with the more intense, or space-invading dog, though I teach each dog to tune out the other, regardless of their role. After a while the dogs stop noticing each other. They go on auto-pilot. We teach them to turn away from, look away, tune out, and to not engage the other dog, and sometimes we teach them to not engage with any dog. Our goal is to lower the intensity between dogs. They don't know why they are tuning the other out, they just do it. Humans need a why. Paraphrasing Victor Frankl in his *Man's Search for Meaning*: (A man who) knows the "why" for his existence will be able to bear almost any "how."[89] Dogs, in contrast, can be shown how without having a why.

I use a similar intervention with fear aggressive and anxious dogs. I teach them to turn away, tune out, "leave it!" in relation to the objects of their fear and anxiety. It's counter-intuitive, but highly effective and confidence-building. Dogs that succeed at letting go of their interest in triggers, such as we saw with Dolly, later are able to interact with the triggers with more calm and confidence.

Where to Find Reliable Information on Aggression

Below are leads to information about the various types of aggression, written by known, reliable sources and available on the Internet at the time of this writing. If this is an area of particular interest, I encourage you to read some of the articles that follow.

....
89   Viktor E. Frankl. E., *Man's Search for Meaning* (New York: Washington Square Press, Simon and Schuster, 1963) 127.

On Aggression

- Search the *DVM Newsmagazine's* Web site, www.dvm360.com.

- Search the Dog Star Daily Web site, www.dogstardaily.com.

- **Bites to Family.** "Dogs that Bite Children: Is There Hope?" article. Behavior Rx Case of the Month for December, 1997. Pet Behavior Resources. www.webtrail.com/petbehavior/dec97. html.

- "Dogs that Bite the Hand that Feeds Them" by Alice Moon-Fanelli, PhD, CAAB, Tufts University School of Veterinary Medicine, North Grafton, MA, USA. Tufts Animal Expo Conference Proceedings, September 1, 2002. www.iknowledgenow.com/ search_form.cfm. (There may be a small charge for this article.)

- **Medical.** Dodman, Nicholas DVM. "Medical Causes of Aggression in Dogs". www.petplace.com.

I explain my approach in greater detail in the "Behavior Cache" section under "Dog-to-Dog Approaches", along with alternative approaches that are being used to help countless dogs. As always, diversity enriches.

SECTION FOUR

BEHAVIOR CACHE

Ali the Airedale Update

At the outset of this book I told you about the Airedale terrier, Ali, who eats pencils, lipsticks and socks. As a reminder, Ali's family had to take him to the animal emergency hospital often and once for surgery to remove an object he ingested. Veterinarians diagnosed him as having everything from an obsessive-compulsive disorder to pica and an irritable bowel.

During my visit to his home, Ali ran and sneaked through the house, grabbing whatever was within reach that he could fit in his mouth. He bolted off with pencils, rocks, lipsticks and socks. He usually found his objects up high, on counters and in containers he ransacked. Living with Ali was like living with a toddler who must be supervised every waking moment.

Ali was the third dog I worked with that presented with pica, "an abnormal appetite or craving for substances that are not fit to eat, such as chalk or clay, common in malnutrition, pregnancy, etc."[90] With all three dogs, the veteri-

90 *Random House Dictionary*, s.v. pica <http://www.dictionary.com>.

narians assessed there might be an underlying medical problem that could not yet be diagnosed.

It could also be in the genes. Recent research does show a genetic link to compulsive behavior in dogs.[91] Dr. Karen Overall, a veterinary behaviorist at the University of Pennsylvania, "suggests that up to 8 percent of dogs in America, five million to six million animals, exhibit compulsive behaviors... Males with the problem outnumber females three to one in dogs...(and) dogs usually developed compulsive behavior between ages 1 and 4."[92] As such, I understood the dog's physiology might be driving his behavior; however, physiology is rarely the sole driver.

Ali was an otherwise well-trained dog with a history that piqued my interest: his family instituted a rule when he was a tiny puppy that he wouldn't be permitted to eat anything but his dog food, ever. The adults thought this was a terrific rule. They'd have no begging from the table. I envisioned him watching longingly as they ate their meals with nothing for him. However, there were elementary-aged and early adolescent children in the family. As such, I assumed the children had at times broken the rule and slipped Ali some food. With the parents present, I asked the children and they denied feeding the dog. "Not me!" When the parents left the room I asked them again and this time they admitted to occasionally feeding Ali from the table and in other rooms when their parents weren't watching. I was pretty sure they fed Ali because this is what children do when parents aren't looking. What surprised me is the children really didn't want their parents to know. Their secrecy created an emotional drama over feeding Ali "illegally". As such, the humans were bringing some of the emotional intensity over food to the situation.

Again, it matters that we assess client situations from different angles. Dogs are scavengers and Ali may have had especially strong drives for scavenging. Perhaps his brain functioned in such a way that he was more apt than other dogs to develop obsessions and compulsions, so normal scavenging could

91 N. H. Dodman, E. K. Karlsson, A. Moon-Fanelli, M. Galdzicka, M. Perloski, L. Shuster, K. Lindblad-Toh and E. I. Ginns. "A canine chromosome 7 locus confers compulsive disorder susceptibility". *Molecular Psychiatry* 15 (2010): 8 10; doi:10.1038/mp.2009.111.

92 Mark Derr. "Scientists Find a Shared Gene in Dogs With Compulsive Behavior", *New York Times* (January 18, 2010).

easily evolve into an obsessive-compulsive disorder. Whatever the case, I thought we could help him by limiting his freedom to get to illegals and giving him opportunities to scavenge for "legal" and good-tasting foods that would be better for him than such objects as makeup and pens. As such, we had to break the family's rule of "no people food for Ali."

We started out by conditioning Ali to want the Super-Motivating treats (recipe and protocol at the end of this section). He was immediately enthralled with them. Next we contained him in a small "safe room" (with nothing that could be ingested) while we planted Super-Motivating treats throughout the house, as treasures. I wanted to draw him away from looking up high and get him hooked on searching at floor level instead. As such, we placed the Super-Motivating treats on (inedible) plates, on floors in every room Ali normally had access to.

Ali loved the Super-Motivating treats and delighted in hunting for them throughout the house. After one run he transitioned from looking up high to looking down for his treasures. (Note: We had to consult first with his veterinarian about limiting the ingredients used in his treats because he had an irritable bowel presumably brought on by eating, as you might guess, non-food junk.)

The intervention worked and within a few days Ali was interested in finding the treats, which he gobbled down on the spot. He was not interested in the non-nutritive/non-tasty stuff that used to catch his attention. Furthermore, when he was not scavenging for treats he was tethered to a family member and could not get to other objects.

This intervention gave us a new beginning and Ali was thrilled with it. Gradually, the family tapered off the planting of "legal" treats by putting less out, less often. In addition, they started planting treats in the small "safe room" I described above. When he could not find treats planted throughout the house, he could sometimes find them in the safe room.

The family was committed to creating opportunities for Ali to scavenge "legally". They agreed to let the children slip Ali food so Ali the Scavenger could have regular conquests! New habits replaced old habits and, while Ali remained a high-maintenance dog, the family reported there were no additional trips to the emergency room to unclog his gastrointestinal plumbing.

Dietary Protein & Aggression

The families I work with complete a behavior questionnaire that I review before I meet with them. You never know when some small scrap of information will change the diagnostic picture. One area of import is diet. What do their dogs eat? If the family lists a food I haven't researched in the past, I search for the nutrition label on the Internet, or ask to see food bags in the dog's home. The lower-caliber foods give cause for concern I've learned to read food labels from my own struggles to diet and live healthy. Ingredients listed first are most prevalent; if the first ingredient is corn, for example, you have a problem. Would you want corn as the mainstay of *your* diet? In the past, high protein foods were thought to cause aggression, though studies showing a correlation between high dietary protein and aggression have been drawn into question in recent years, and most veterinary behaviorists are not now recommending that we reduce protein content as a strategy to manage aggression.

The most cited study that shows a correlation between high dietary protein and aggression concludes (in the year 2000), "although the current evidence is equivocal with respect to the benefits of a diet containing reduced dietary protein for managing (aggression), preliminary veterinary data suggest that some dogs exhibiting territorial aggression with fear may benefit from a low protein diet . . . especially when it is supplemented with tryptophan"[93]

A decade ago, veterinary behaviorist Dr. Bonnie Beaver summarized the above study as follows: "Dietary protein has specifically been linked to two

....
93   J. S. DeNapoli., N. H. Dodman, et al. "Effect of dietary protein content and tryptophan supplementation on dominance aggression, territorial aggression, and hyperactivity in dogs". *Journal of the American Veterinary Medical Association* 217(4) (Aug 15, 2000):504-08.

undesirable behaviors: fear aggression and territorial aggression. Both behaviors decrease when dietary protein is lowered from 3-18%. It is hypothesized that low-protein diets facilitate the conversion of tryptophan to serotonin, which in turn reduces the impulsivity of fearful dogs."[94]

It's not a simple issue and needs to be more thoroughly researched. I want to know if there are differences between protein delivered through lower caliber processed dog food, and protein from solid meat sources such as human-grade chicken, fish or beef. In addition, some of the highest caliber dry dog foods rely on top sources of protein such as wild Salmon and naturally grown chicken. The protein percentages may be high but with zero correlation with aggression for dogs eating these foods. As such, I'm more concerned when the low-grade foods are high in protein. It's quite possible that good quality protein contributes, not to aggression, but to calming dogs. Life is full of such ambiguities and paradoxes, which is why I recommend against investing too fervently in one's beliefs of the moment.

I do elect to make information about diet and protein available to veterinarians and families whose dogs are on low caliber, high protein foods, and some who change to higher caliber foods report a lessening of reactivity and aggression when they switch. However, by the time they have changed foods it's difficult to tell how much effect is from food and how much from the behavior modification plan that's already been implemented.

....
94   Beaver. *Canine Behavior*, 260.

Digging & Lawn Problems

Lawns

If your dog's activities are a threat to the well-being of your lawn, I recommend you read the "Dog-On-It Lawn Problems" article, posted to the Internet. It first appeared in the Web issue of *Horticulture Update* in 2002, edited by Dr. Douglas Welsh.[95] You will find online an updated version of the original:

Article: Lawn Problems

'Dog-On-It' Lawn Problems, Updated

---

95 *Horticulture Update* in 2002 , ed. Dr. Douglas Welsh, Extension Horticulture, Texas Cooperative Extension, Texas A&M University System, College Station, Texas. <http://www.Aggiehorticulture.tamu.edu/extension/newsletters/jhortupdate/jun02/art2jun.html>.

Aggiehorticulture.tamu.edu/extension/newsletters/jhortupdate/jun02/art2jun.html

One of the simplest solutions is to teach dogs to eliminate in a small, non-essential area of the lawn. With newly adopted dogs and puppies, this can be accomplished by taking dogs out on-leash for as long as it takes, and rewarding them for eliminating in human-sanctioned areas.

Problems with Digging

Terriers are typically excited by scents and happily dig at holes in the ground to search for little critters. Other dogs like to bury treasures. On hot summer days some cool off in their holes, or dig because they are bored or anxious. For some, a hole is more simply to dig. Most worrisome is when dogs dig so they can escape.

There's something care-taking we can do for our digger dogs and our yards: build a dig box, or space in the yard, and establish that it's "legal" to dig there. Legal dig spots may not completely solve your problem, but they can take the edge off of dog's zest for digging in "illegal" spots.

How to Build "Legal" Dig Spots

- Be creative and tailor these instructions to the soil or surface you have to work with. Watch how your dog digs to understand how much space and depth he needs.

- Find a suitable spot in the yard. Legal spots should not be located near a fence line—we don't want to encourage dogs to dig their way to freedom!

- Loosen the soil in the area, as if you were preparing a flower bed. Vermiculite is a usable material and it's cleaner than some of the alternatives. You shouldn't need one of the finer grades but check with a garden supply store to match the vermiculite to your soil and your purpose. You could mix it in with good garden soil, and possibly some sand. Sand's drawback is that it sticks to damp paws and can be tracked through the house.

- If your ground is difficult to till, you can build a dig box, several feet above ground level and three feet square or more, depending on the size of your dog and your dog's stance when digging. You can use weatherproofed railroad ties or even a swimming pool made with heavy plastic that will hold up over time and can be stored when the weather is severe. Loosen the soil beneath the dig box as much as possible before filling the box with a mix of vermiculite, garden soil, and sand.

- Next, hide interesting toys and bones in the dig box. You might have to help your dog get started but once a dog unearths his first treasure, he's usually sold on legal dig spots.

- In the beginning, you will have to bury good stuff in the dig box every day, perhaps several times a day, then taper off to every few days, then once a week, to once every two weeks. If your dog is very serious about digging, why not continue burying items in the box, as needed to sustain his habit, for the digging life of the dog?

It hopefully goes without saying at this point that telling dogs "No! No dig!" or punishing them for digging won't solve the problem. The overriding principle is, "Give them something else to do."

Dog-to-Dog Approaches

We all know of dogs that growl and lunge when they are in proximity to other dogs, similar to Murphy and the dog aggressive Labrador discussed in my introduction. Dog aggressive dogs are of course not all the same—not in intensity, seriousness of purpose, "trigger distance" (how close do they have to be to another dog before they become aroused and sound off), likes and dislikes (does any dog encountered trigger a response or just small dogs, or big dogs, or dogs of a particular breed, dogs on leash, dogs that are also reactive, etc..), resource guarding (does the dog only aggress when protecting a high-value resource (such as a family member, or a bone), and so on.

With all this variability, we have a wide variety of approaches to choose from when we're searching for strategies to help dogs handle encounters with other dogs, or any "Scary Others". I outline four approaches below.

STRATEGY ONE:

OPTING OUT
Lynn Hoover, MSW

When dog's typical response is to dramatize their encounters with "triggers", an empathic connection to this fascinating species leads me to conclude that being all strung out doesn't feel very good, though it probably confers some release, akin to what sports fans feel when they've yelled and screamed their way through games of "us" vs. "them". My intent, therefore, is to teach dogs that if they just let go/tune out ("Opting Out") they'll get really good stuff and will feel better overall, much better than they feel during fractious encounters with "Scary Ones".

I want to clarify a point that's illustrated in my case studies: my approach to modifying aggression is a very distant cousin to obedience training. I understand that desensitization and counterconditioning are taking place. But I don't want dogs thinking (in dog picture language) "what does she want from me and should I say 'yes'?" I simply supply powerful conditioned reinforcers, such as Super-Motivating treats, that naturally trump the reinforcement dogs get when they 'sound off' and go after other dogs and people.

Dog's other option, the one they've selected in the past, has been to pay far too much attention to the object of their fears; some escalate to warfare. I show them an alternative: if they let go, tune out and redirect their attention to conditioned super-motivating reinforcers, not only do good things happen in the form of reinforcers, but they *feel* better than before.

I illustrate again here how empathy can be employed as a powerful tool if we can stop marginalizing discussions of animal's emotions. Most humans have figured out that calm feels better than storms. We are inundated with advertising that encourages us to seek relaxation for better long-term health and more feel-good moments. Reactive dogs don't have insight about relaxation. As such, I coach families to woo their dogs and draw them to experience the joys of letting go of old response habits, i.e. they replace tuning in and paying way too much attention to "Scary Ones" with new habits of non-engagement.

As dogs become more proficient at letting go, they grow in confidence; the appearance of "Scary Ones" is no longer a threat to them. They know exactly what to do: invisibilize what they fear.

"Opting Out" restores families to calm as well. I ask families to divert their dogs when they are just beginning to become aroused but before they're fully reactive because once they're reactive it's too late; see Brenda Aloff's protocols below to understand this phenomenon. If we divert attention prematurely, i.e. before dogs even notice a "Scary One", they're not apt to learn anything about letting go.

When families are wooing their dogs I ask them to not correct the dogs for unwanted behaviors. If they aren't being reactive, let them move about naturally, without interference.

In the case study section of this book, Murphy's person erred when she insisted that Murphy heel when he wanted to sniff and run around as a replacement for tuning in to movement by neighboring dogs.

I worked with a dog who was excessively tuned in and anxious about visitors. When her people diverted her, she let go of her interest in the "Scary Ones", i.e. like me, and found something else to do: she put her dear, gangly, adolescent paws up on a counter to look longingly at a fresh-roasted rotisserie chicken I'd planted there. Her people corrected her. I asked her family, "would you rather have a dog who puts herself up high so she can see what's going on up there, or a dog that goes after visitors? Dogs that bite visitors are apt to lose their homes and possibly their lives; "counter-viewing" (I wouldn't characterize her behavior as "counter-surfing" as yet) doesn't typically result in ostracism. Worry about counter behavior later, when I'm not here."

STRATEGY TWO:
"LOOK AT THAT" GAME
Leslie McDevitt, MLA

Leslie McDevitt is an accomplished clicker trainer and author of *Control Unleashed: Creating a Focused and Confident Dog (2007)*. She published several DVD's that are apt to especially hit the spot for visual learners. The book and DVDs can be purchased through Dogwise, www.dogwise.com.

Essentially, with McDevitt's approach, we wait for dogs to looks at "Scary Ones". When they look, we click. When dogs hear the click they turn back to us, because they know from the click that a treat is coming. They have a new experience of looking at "Scary Ones" that typically cause them to feel anxious and distressed, but the outcome is better. This intervention stems from McDevitt's view of reactivity as an "information-seeking strategy". So if we let reactive dogs get the information they seek and then return their attention to us, they become less reactive to their triggers. As ex plained by Dr. Dani Weinberg, an experienced dog behavior consultant and clicker training instructor in Albuquerque, New Mexico, they become no longer interested in the "Scary Thing" except as an indirect source of cookies.

The approach requires that dogs are taught foundation behaviors first. To understand the approach with sufficient depth to use it effectively, I recommend you read or view some of McDevitt's publications. Many of my colleagues find McDevitt's approach helpful, simple and relatively easy to apply.

When I reinforce dogs for looking at "Scary Things", it's for different reasons that are tied to my assessment of family systems. If a reactive dog's family has been hauling him away at the first sign of trouble, I go counter to the family's typical response and help the dog achieve peace through looking at but not being "defeated" by "Scary Things". As a family therapist, I learned how to unbalance systems and their old, dysfunctional patterns by employing interventions that run counter to the same-old, same-old that families have been employing and account for a stagnant homeostasis, or sameness, in systems.

I understand from trainers who use "Look at That" regularly, it's a powerful intervention that enhances dog's confidence, just as my "Opting Out" strategy enhances dog's confidence, but in a different way.

STRATEGY THREE:
CONSTRUCTIONAL AGGRESSION TREATMENT (CAT)
Jesus Rosales-Ruiz, PhD & Kellie Snider, MS

Dr. Jesus Rosales-Ruiz and Kellie Snider developed an innovative approach to shaping dogs away from their aggression. You'll find their book and DVD's at Dogwise, www.dogwise.com. The approach is described on Dogwise as follows: "C.A.T. is a functional approach to changing aggressive behavior. It acknowledges that the dog is already receiving reinforcement for aggression and sets up a procedure in which the same reinforcer that currently supports the aggression is arranged to follow only desirable, safe behaviors. As the procedure progresses, the ultimate outcome is a once-aggressive dog that is now friendly."

On the Tawzer Web site, "Constructional Aggression Treatment" is described as "a controversial new procedure". I and many of my colleagues have helped dogs using this approach and the changes have held. In my opinion, it's too complex to be used casually; it may require a sophisticated understanding of the underlying principles of applied behavior analysis and the methods set forth by Rosales-Ruiz and Snider. I recommend beginners read Dr. Jon Bailey and Dr. Mary Burch's 2006 book, *How to Think Like a Behavior Analyst*[96], or a similar basic text before tackling "Constructional Aggression Treatment".

STRATEGY FOUR:

DOG-TO-DOG APPROACHES
Brenda Aloff

The protocols described below were designed by a highly experienced behavior consultant and trainer in Midland, Michigan, Brenda Aloff.[97] I recommend anyone serious about modifying aggression read her book, even those who prefer using some of the more recently developed strategies described above. I've relied on variations of Aloff's instructions for going on ten years. They are published in Aloff's classic, *Aggression in Dogs*. The book, at over 400 pages, is full of insights and strategies for dealing with aggression.

Dog-to-Dog Approaches

Goal: Your dog will allow other dogs to pass by and near him without barking, lunging and growling, or becoming so aroused he can't pay attention to you.

What it teaches: Other dogs are not dangerous. It's not his business to run over and kick everybody's butt.

....

96   Bailey, Jon, PhD, and M. Burch, PhD. How to Think Like a Behavior Analyst. Lawrence Erlbaum Assoc., 2006.

97   Aloff, *Aggression in Dogs.Practical Management Prevention and Behaviour Modification*. Dogwise Publishing, 2001. Brenda Aloff 's Web site: <http://www.brendaaloff.com>

Desensitization program: Don't place your dog in circumstances beyond his current skill level, or yours. Aggression, in many cases, is merely a symptom of anxiety and fear. Only your dog can determine the rate at which he can learn new coping mechanisms to stem underlying anxiety and fear. At the same time, while proceeding patiently, you must make sure you are raising criteria, therefore creating opportunities to reinforce even more desirable behaviors. It's also important to know your dog and to have done enough training with the dog so you make the right moves to obtain the behavior or to apply damage control to the various difficulties that come up.

If lack of self-confidence or lack of education are at the heart of the aggression, then anxiety and fear are probably the core causative factors.

Whether fear, anxiety, relationship issues, or some other concern is contributing to the problems you are facing with your dog, you must complete your "homework" before beginning this protocol. This means you have achieved fluency with foundation behaviors: going into this you must have good stimulus control with cues such as "Leave It" and "Attention" (call dog's name, dog tunes into you). Success is defined as having no aggressive events, and little to no reaction from your dog.

Source of problem: Mostly, it's just not clear to the dog that defaulting to the environment, instead of the owner/handler, is incorrect. The dog has a deep-seated habit defaulting to the environment and responding with knee-jerk arousal to environmental stimuli. This habit has been in place for so long it's very difficult to interrupt when you first begin to do so. He's been allowed to practice the undesired behavior. The dog is not including you in his decision-making process.

So, work on basic behaviors, and then begin to intervene as follows:

First determine the threshold at which your dog reacts to other dogs. At what point does he spot another dog and begin to exhibit signs of body tension, nervousness or hyperactivity? Is it eight feet or thirty feet? You'll start at a distance just prior to the distance at which your dog begins to react with obvious signs of growling, barking and lunging. To begin at a distance at which some slight body tension and even a slight pilo-erector reflex are evident is acceptable.

From this distance, begin to recognize the first signs your dog uses to indicate he's "On Alert". When you're working with dogs that have been over-reactive or aggressive with other dogs, it's critical that you understand the importance of "Alerting", and can recognize it quickly. Alerting is the point at which the dog is beginning to get fired up. For dogs that are going to react inappropriately, this is a crucial moment. If you don't respond to this Alerting behavior in your dog, he may assume you approve of what he's doing and will "back him up." If you don't notice an Alerting event and let it slide by, you are, in your dog's paradigm, directly giving him permission to follow through with his current thoughts and become more reactive. If you are going to modify this dog's behavior, when the dog Alerts is the optimum time to intervene. Remember: once past this state and into a stage of more intense reaction (lunging, barking, snarling, and growling), you're merely practicing damage control and are not modifying behavior at all (at least, not in the direction you want to go!).

At the first signs of Alerting, you'll use your "Move Away" from it exercise. Just move away or, better yet, in the "Acquisition Stage of Learning", "Back Away" from the dog your dog is Alerting on. Don't dawdle. Move backwards quickly, but smoothly. When you do this Back Away, remain neutral. (I know, easier said than done, but it's possible. So do it.) Emotionality or anger on your part will merely validate your dog's point of view that other dogs are bad news and always cause trouble. Correcting your dog or yelling at him will exacerbate this behavior, again by validating your dog's current paradigm that every time another dog appears, you become upset, nervous and occasionally attack him.

The moment your dog turns toward you, reinforce him. Continue to back up two or three more steps, using verbal encouragement to keep your dog moving toward you. As your dog reaches you, "Mark It & Feed It". Deliver a "Jackpot" (a really good reward such as a Super-Motivating treat) for first "Correct Efforts". After the first couple of Correct Efforts, set one threshold distance, Mark It & Feed It, then resume work by decreasing the threshold distance.

Each time you decrease the threshold distance, remember, you'll receive a first Correct Effort at that closer distance. Jackpot it accordingly, then move to a variable schedule of reinforcement. This means you'll stop reinforcing every time you get the behavior you want and instead reinforce him intermittently. You change the frequency gradually. For example, you would at first reward your dog for every "good" (human-preferred) behavior, and then reward every other time, then every third time, and so on until the dog is rewarded randomly and the new habit holds even when the dog is not getting rewards. If you don't switch over to random reinforcements your dog will expect rewards for "good" behavior, for the rest of his life.

A qualified behaviorist, behavior consultant or trainer would help you carry out any of the protocols introduced above. It's usually a challenge to get the timing right, and moreso, to figure out how to bring about change without stressing dogs or their interlocking systems. (See "Professional Matters" in "Section Three: All That Matters" about the challenge of finding qualified professionals in your community.)

Dominance

Many dog families I encounter (and their veterinarians), think dogs are trying to dominate them when the dogs are, in my view, expressing fear and anxiety or are driven by needs and innate drives that have absolutely nothing to do with dominance. As illustrated elsewhere in my book, this leads them to wrong conclusions about what they must do to change their dog's behavior. In essence, how can they meet their dog's needs if they don't understand them?

The resources listed in this section will hopefully interest readers with suspicions about their dog's intentions, and those who are curious about the dominance paradigm and why it's fallen into such disfavor with behavior professionals.

I'll clarify here that I believe some dogs do show what can rightfully be termed "dominance". It's not politically correct for me to admit to this, just as it's not politically correct to admit publicly that some Pit bulls are danger-ous and their aggression is not owner or handler-created. And, as Morgan Spector explains in his article below on dominance myths: "Some dogs have more assertive personalities than others."[98] The key point is that assertiveness met by force can result in aggression.

Let's take a look at the "Position Statement on the Use of Dominance Theory in Behavior Modification of Animals", published by the American Veterinary Society of Animal Behavior (AVSAB).

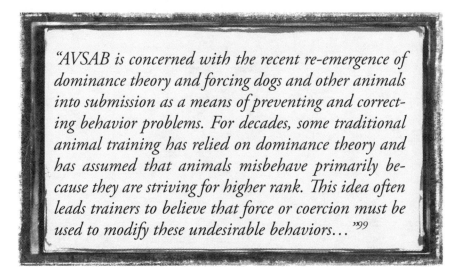

"AVSAB is concerned with the recent re-emergence of dominance theory and forcing dogs and other animals into submission as a means of preventing and correct-ing behavior problems. For decades, some traditional animal training has relied on dominance theory and has assumed that animals misbehave primarily be-cause they are striving for higher rank. This idea often leads trainers to believe that force or coercion must be used to modify these undesirable behaviors... "[99]

To broaden your perspective, I recommend you also read Dr. Sophia Yin's ar-ticle, "Experts Say Dominance-Based Dog Training Techniques Made Popular By Television Shows Can Contribute to Dog Bites".[100] Dr. Yin is a veterinar-ian and applied animal behaviorist practicing in San Francisco.[101] In another

98   Morgan Spector, "Moving Beyond the Dominance Myth: Toward an Understanding of Training as Partnership." (2001)

99   For a full statement published on the Internet, go to <http://www.AVSABonline.org>, click on AVSAB Position Statements on the left bar, then Dominance Position Statement .

100   Sophia Yin, DVM. "Experts Say Dominance-Based Dog Training Techniques Made Popular By Television Shows Can Contribute to Dog Bites". *Huffington Post,* (May 18, 2009). <http:www.huffingtonpost.com>.

101   Sophia Yin, DVM, <http://www.AskDrYin.com>.

article, Dr. John Ciribassi, a veterinary behaviorist practicing in Chicago and a past-president of the American Veterinary Society of Animal Behavior, posits as follows about dogs aggressive to strangers: "Initially the dog barks at people as they pass and backs away if approached, indicating that the aggression is due to fear. The owner is referred to a trainer or watches a show that demonstrates the use of a choke chain or pinch collar and verbal or physical corrections. Because the dog now feels pain when it encounters the person it fears, the aggression escalates (and) now the dog lunges, snaps, and bites in situations where it used to bark and back away…"[102]

You hopefully see why dominance theory has fallen into such disrepute among informed behaviorists and trainers. I encourage academics to read the article published below with permission from it's author, Morgan Spector, an attorney, writer and accomplished clicker trainer in Palmdale, California.

Additional articles written by reliable sources are on the Web, as follows:

Dominance and Related Articles

"Whatever Happened to the Term Alpha Wolf?" by David L. Mech, <http://www.wolf.org/wolves/news/iwmag/2008/winter/alphawolf.pdf>

Interview with David L. Mech, <http://www.youtube.com/watch?v=tNtFgdwTsbU>

"Debunking the Dominance Myth" by Pamela Buitrago, CPDT

"The History and Misconceptions of Dominance Theory" by Melissa Alexander <http://www.clickersolutions.com/articles/index.htm#dominance>

Again, Dr. Yin's "Experts Say Dominance-Based Dog Training Techniques Made Popular By Television Shows Can Contribute to Dog Bites" <http:www.huffingtonpost.com>

---

101. John Ciribassi in article by Sophia Yin, DVM. "Dominance-Based Dog Training Techniques", *Huffington Post*, (May 18, 2009). Web site < http://www.chicagovetbehavior.com/>

Dominance Article
by Morgan Spector

MOVING BEYOND THE DOMINANCE MYTH:

TOWARD AN UNDERSTANDING OF TRAINING
AS PARTNERSHIP

OVERVIEW

Dog trainers have commonly accepted a model of training based on a supposed emulation of the behaviors of wolves, particularly Alpha wolves. Central to this model is the notion of "dominance". This model is conceptually flawed in that it rests on some serious misconceptions about wolf behavior as well as serious misconceptions about the interactions between dogs and humans. As a separate species from dogs, humans cannot emulate intraspecific behaviors and expect those behaviors to be interpreted other than as aggression. A more accurate and ultimately more productive training model is to approach training from the point of view of symbiosis: interspecific cooperation based on some form of mutual benefit.

BACKGROUND: THE ROOTS OF TRADITIONAL TRAINING

Dog training has long been characterized by a tendency toward the use of force and compulsion. For example, Most explains the basis of training this way:

- *"What is the actual object of training? It is that the dog shall only do what we find convenient or useful, and refrain from doing what is inconvenient or harmful to us. This requirement cannot be completely reconciled with what is acceptable by, or of advantage to, the dog.*

- *"It is only when a dog learns that the adoption or abandonment, disagreeable in themselves, of certain action will be to his own advantage that training can be proceeded with on a sound basis. Such is the object of compulsion." (Most, pp. 24-25)*

This view did not change substantially from 1910 when Most first published his book through the 1960s when Koehler wrote his basic training guide. Koehler expressed his philosophy this way:

- *"Magazines have dignified the prattle of 'dog psychologists' who would rob the dog of a birthright he has in common with all of God's creatures: the right to the consequences of his own action.*

There will always be more emphasis and clarity to be had in the contrast between punishment and reward than from the technique of 'only good' and if they obey, 'still more good.' And there is more meaning and awareness of life that knows the consequences of both favorable and unfavorable action. So let's not deprive the dog of his privilege of experiencing the consequences of right and wrong, or, more definitely, punishment as well as praise." (Koehler, p. 21)

Their differences notwithstanding (Most, for example, rejected an anthropomorphic view of dogs while Koehler, as evidenced by the above quote, tended toward an anthropomorphic view) Koehler and Most both assumed that humans in some way had the right to compel dogs to act in certain ways acceptable to humans. For Most the basis of this is clear: he was one of the first people to train dogs for military and police work. Koehler's books were written for the more general public pet-owning population. The implicit assumption in Koehler's work is clear but unstated: dogs live in human society and must follow human rules, and humans must use compulsion to get dogs to follow those rules. But there was more than that. There was a further view that the use of compulsion in training elevated the dog. This extension of Koehler's implicit anthropomorphism took full flight in Vicki Hearne, who presents as one of Koehler's leading acolytes. Hearne argues that:

- *"Koehler holds, against the skepticism that in the last two centuries has become largely synonymous with philosophy, that getting absolute obedience from a dog – and he means absolute – confers nobility, character and dignity on the dog" (Hearne, p. 41).*

Yet neither Koehler's straightforward, hard-boiled program nor Hearne's pedagogical flights of fancy gave any meaningful answer to the underlying question: what in fact gives humans the right to inflict training methods on dogs that can only be described as unremittingly harsh and physically punishing? Far from conferring "nobility, character and dignity on the dog" the methods in fact give the dog no room at all to be anything but an absolutely subservient being under constant pain of punishment.

DOMINANCE: THE ETHOLOGICAL SHEEP IN WOLVES' CLOTHING

Enter the Monks of New Skete. The Monks' work was considered quite progressive. For purposes of this discussion however, the Monks were the first modern trainers to articulate a clear theoretical basis for the use of compulsion in training. Their model was the wolf pack (at least, the wolf pack as they understood it). They wrote "To learn about dogs, learn about wolves." And they wrote:

- *". . . "[W]olf and dog have striking similarities. Both are innately pack-oriented and prefer not to be isolated for long periods of time. . . . Both are responsive to leadership from an 'Alpha-figure' to whom they look for order and directives." (Monks at 12)*

The monks assert the theory:

- *"[S]ince we have deprived the dog, through domestication, of its normal pack life, the dog has adopted us as its new pack. A dog perceives the people it lives with as fellow-members of a pack. Once a dog understands this, he can understand training methods that, while including the dog in the pack, lower the dog in the pecking order." (Monks at 13, emphasis added)*

This is the underlying rationale for what has come to be known as "dominance" theory: Dogs see themselves as living in a pack with humans, therefore humans have to emulate pack behavior and, specifically, assume the Alpha position within the pack. Ironically, although the direct analogy to wolves was new, the notion of dogs and humans forming a pack in which humans must reign supreme was not. Most articulated the same theory in 1910. He wrote:

- *"In a pack of young dogs fierce fights take place to decide how they are to rank within the pack. And in a pack composed of men and dogs, canine competition for importance in the eyes of the trainer is keen. . . . As in a pack of dogs, the order of hierarchy in a man and dog combination can only be established by physical force, that is by an actual struggle, in which the man is instantly victorious. Such a result can only be brought about by convincing the dog of the absolute physical superiority of the man. Otherwise the dog will lead and the man follow. If a dog shows the slightest sign of rebellion against his trainer or leader, the physical superiority of the man as leader of the pack must be given instant expression in the most unmistakable manner." (Most at 13, emphasis added)*

Based on the notion that dogs and humans form a unitary pack in which humans must rule, "dominance" becomes the central issue in the relationship between human and canine. This "dominance paradigm" may be said to underlie all approaches to training rooted in the use of force to compel obedience. Disobedience is not merely a failure to perform a behavior when called upon to do so, but incipient rebellion against the Alpha. As Most put it:

- *"Should a dog rebel against his trainer, instant resort to severe compulsion is essential. . . . For, each time the dog finds that he is not instantly mastered, the canine competitive instinct will increase and his submissive instinct will weaken. One of the objects of training, however, is to inculcate the reverse condition." (Most, 35-36)*

There are several fallacies in this paradigm although there is a kernel of truth within it. The kernel of truth is that dogs must live appropriately within human society, both in the home and in the world at large, and that humans are responsible for teaching dogs how to do so through training. But there is no need for a theory of "dominance" to explain the need for this training. And seeing the purpose of training as achieving "dominance" sets up an approach to training that all too easily becomes unduly harsh and punishing. As noted, punitive methods are justified by the logic of the "pack" approach.

DOMINANCE AS A PRODUCT OF INTRASPECIFIC AGGRESSION

It is important to understand what "dominance" represents in the natural order. Lindsay explains that dominance is a product of a certain type of aggression occurring within members of the same species (or, intraspecific aggression). He writes:

- *"In general intraspecific aggression provides a countervailing and distance-increasing function over place and social attachment processes but without breaking down affiliative contact altogether. As such, ritualized intraspecific aggression imposes social order (e.g., the formation of a dominance hierarchy) and territorial limits on the interaction between individuals belonging to the same species." (Lindsay, p. 167).*

- *Lindsay distinguishes intraspecific from interspecific aggression, pointing out that "Interspecific aggression refers to aggressive behavior directed against another species and includes both offensive and defensive elements. Although intraspecific aggression is most often associated with competition between closely socialized animals belonging to the same species, interspecific aggression is most frequently associated with self-protective goals, as, for example, occur when a prey animal defends itself against the attack of a predator. The dog's relationship with humans is complex in this regard, with both competitive and self-protective aggression being exhibited under different situations." (Ibid.)*

We can understand the fallacies of the dominance paradigm if we first understand that "dominance" is really a set of behaviors that can be identified and therefore can be modified. And in almost all cases this set of behaviors exists within a larger range of social behaviors available to and exhibited by the dog within the context of social relationships within which the dog functions.

Seen from this perspective, the first major fallacy in the "dominance paradigm" is to regard the dog-inclusive family as a canine "pack". The second major fallacy is to classify a given dog as "dominant". Related to this is the third major fallacy, seeing "dominance" as though it were a psychological disorder or condition rather than a set of behaviors exhibited by the dog in response to the situation in which he lives.

FALLACY ONE: THAT THE DOG-INCLUSIVE FAMILY IS TRULY A "PACK"

Dogs and humans are alien to each other and our societies have different rules and mores. If our household were in fact a canine pack then we should have to expect to live by dogs' rules, and that is clearly impossible. Dogs must live by human rules, which means that dogs have to surrender their ordinary modes of interaction insofar as they are interacting with humans and not other dogs.

- This fact alone tells us that our relationship with our dogs is not intraspecific but interspecific. The same actions which if directed by one member of a given species against another member of that species would lead to some settling of hierarchy and order take on a far different quality when directed by a member of one species against a member of another species. As Lindsay suggests, our acts of physical "discipline" are in fact a form of interspecific aggression.

While acknowledging that a group of dogs remaining together for any length of time can form a stable hierarchy, Dunbar tells us:

- *We should also recognize that nobody really knows what is meant by the word "dominant". "Dominance" has become a catch phrase to cover a wide range of behaviors and so-called "attitudes", many of which can be best explained or understood without any reference to "dominance". We have much the same problem with terms such as "aggression" and "submission". The problem is exemplified by the evolution of phrases such as "submissive aggression" that almost defies explanation.*

- *"To say that the hierarchy is the sole basis of dog social behavior would be incorrect. The notion of hierarchies has been much over-played. For the most part, dogs seem to live in relative harmony with each member of the group, each generally going about its business with an apparent disinterest in the affairs of others." (Dunbar, p. 85)*

At most the "pack" concept is of some limited metaphorical value. It does not even necessarily accurately express the range of behaviors within a given association of wolves (Coppinger, pp. 66-67). It cannot be a basis for understanding the interaction between humans and dogs, much less for establishing a training approach.

FALLACY TWO: CLASSIFYING A GIVEN DOG AS "DOMINANT".

This kind of classification is a human tendency but it ignores the realities of canine identity and interaction. Dogs are social and interactive animals and are very responsive to their circumstances. Dunbar tells us

- *"The traditional notion of interaction between dogs is one of a dyadic dominant/subordinate relationship. This is to say that when two dogs encounter each other, one dominates the other. This is a useful framework for an initial analysis, but again it is far too simple and rigid to fully explain a complex situation." (Dunbar, 88)*

Any given dog may be dominant or compliant at any given time depending on the situation. The apparently "subordinate" dog may in fact control many interactions (Dunbar, 88-89). It is true that some dogs have more assertive personalities than others, but for training purposes it does not help to classify such a dog as "dominant". The dog with the strongest (i.e., most "dominant") personality may also be the most compliant with training as well as the most willing worker.

FALLACY THREE: THAT "DOMINANCE" IS A PATHOLOGY RATHER THAN A BEHAVIOR OR SET OF BEHAVIORS WHICH CAN BE IDENTIFIED AND THEREFORE MODIFIED

"Dominance" is considered a problem trait and becomes the prism through which we view a given dog, much the same as if we were to say of a human that he is "a borderline personality" or "manic depressive". If "dominance" is some sort of underlying pathology, then how can the trainer deal with it? We cannot put the dog on the couch. All we can do is suppress the dog's dominant tendencies (assuming for the sake of discussion that this is really possible), and this leads ineluctably to physical punishment.

In this vein it should not be surprising that the Monks devote 5 pages of their book to praise (Monks, pp. 36-40) and 11 pages to physical discipline (Monks, pp. 40-50), giving thorough instruction on the mechanics of striking the dog under the chin, the "shakedown" (scruff shake) and the Alpha Wolf Roll-Over. Ironically, as Lindsay notes, this sort of action is likely to be perceived by the dog as physical threats, triggering even stronger aggressive reactions (Lindsay at 168).

But assuming that a given dog has not become sociopathic, what may be termed "dominance" is in fact behavior, that is, a set of things that the dog does. We can identify these behaviors. They may include such things as growling, or shoving into another's space, or object-guarding. Once the behavior is identified, the trainer can modify those behaviors. The trainer can shape incompatible behaviors and otherwise set up a framework to subject the undesirable behaviors to extinction.

ALTERNATIVES TO TRAINING BASED ON "DOMINANCE"

There is an alternative to the "dominance" paradigm. This alternative rests on several perceptions, some of which are at least implicit in what had been set out above.

DOGS ARE NOT HUMANS

First, humans are not dogs and dogs are not humans. We cannot interact with dogs as though we were dogs. Our interactions are interspecific, and in our interactions we must respect the realities that distinguish humans and dogs.

Dogs are social and interactive creatures. Dogs are much better at lubricating their interactions with other dogs than humans are at lubricating interactions with other humans. It is the human lack of sensitivity to social signals that underlies much of our misunderstanding of what canine social behavior is about. For example, if two dogs meet one another and one averts its eyes, this is "good manners" – a canine calming signal that will help avoid any clash between the dogs. If two humans meet one another and one averts his eyes, this suggests shiftiness or a lack of openness. If a human meets a dog and the dog turns its head, the human may try to get the dog to look him right in the eyes. To the human, this is friendly. To the dog, it is antagonistic.

We will interact best if we focus on behavior and not "attitude".

Second, we will do best if we understand that what concerns us is the behavior that the dog produces at any given time. There may be some value in trying to determine the source of that behavior, but such analysis is often speculative and therefore may not be of much use in figuring out how to modify the behavior in question. For example, one may diagnose a certain type of behavior as "predatory", but having done so we have not necessarily clarified our options (although the fact that a given dog consistently manifests predatory behavior may affect our assessment of whether the dog can continue to live in a given family environment).

THE MODEL FOR INTERSPECIFIC INTERACTION IS SYMBIOSIS NOT DOMINANCE

Webster's New World Dictionary defines "symbiosis" as "the intimate living together of two kinds of organisms, especially if such association is of mutual advantage." Although in some ways inexact, this describes a more appropriate paradigm for the relationship between dogs and humans. There is mutual practical advantage in the relationship between dogs and humans. Dogs have their survival needs met; humans can get useful work from dogs. This useful work may consist of actual productive labor (e.g., herding or guarding livestock, hunting, or search and rescue) or it may consist simply of the general psychological and emotional benefits dogs can confer on humans simply by their presence.

Our training should be based on that mutual benefit. Good training effects a "training bargain" in which the human says to the dog "you give me what I want, and I'll give you what you want." The dog, in turn, learns to "say" the same thing to the human. This creates a mutually beneficial partnership in which "dominance" is essentially irrelevant.

Operant conditioning embodies this symbiotic or "partnership" approach. Positive reinforcement is the means for giving the dog what the dog wants, which in turn makes clear to the dog what the human wants by way of behavior. "Dominance" is not an issue. As an operant trainer it is essentially irrelevant to me whether the dog thinks he is "driving" me by using his actions to cause me to click. In fact, in many ways I am perfectly happy that the dog should think so, because that dog has become strongly engaged in the training "game" that we play.

This approach is not only beneficial to the professional or competitive trainer but to the average pet owner as well. In this writer's experience, most pet owners do not want to be in conflict with their dogs and resist harsh training methods. Koehler viewed such people with contempt (see, e.g.: Koehler, pp. 18-19). But in fact it is possible to achieve everything that a trainer wants to achieve, regardless of the type of training involved, through operant conditioning and positive reinforcement. It is not necessary to "dominate" the dog: it is essential to enlist the dog in a cooperative working relationship.

REFERENCES:

Coppinger, Raymond & Lorna. *Dogs – A Startling New Understanding of Canine Origin, Behavior & Evolution.* 2001, Scribner

Dunbar, Dr. Ian. *Dog Behavior – Why Dogs Do What They Do.* TFH Publications

Hearne, Vicki. *Adam's Task: Calling Animals by Name.* Harper Perennial

Koehler, William. *The Koehler Method of Dog Training.* 1962, Howell Book Publishing

Lindsay, Steven R. *Applied Behavior and Dog Training, Vol. II.* 2001, Iowa State University Press

Monks of New Skete. *How To Be Your Dog's Best Friend.* 1978, Little Brown.

Most, Col. Konrad. *Training Dogs – A Manual.* 1954, Popular Dogs Publishing Co. Ltd., London; Reprinted 2000 by Dogwise Publisher.

Morgan Spector is a dog trainer and lawyer practicing in Palmdale, California, and is author of the acclaimed book, *Clicker Training for Obedience: Shaping Top Performance - Positively.* The article above, "Moving Beyond the Dominance Myth: Toward an Understanding of Training as Partnership", is reprinted here with his permission.

Family Systems & Triangulation

> *The self of the blind man includes*
> *the ground he is walking on.*
> Dr. Salvador Minuchin

What follows is a brief discussion of triangulation in families. It is relevant because companion animals are often involved in family struggles.

Have you ever launched into a discussion with a friend, said what you really thought about a controversial issue, expected your perspectives would be the same, then discovered the friend completely disagreed with you? Tensions began to rise but you hit upon a way to handle the discomfort: triangulation. That is, you started complaining about a third person whose ideas were even less appealing, with the advantage that the other person wasn't present to create his own exculpatory triangle.

Triangulation involves pulling in a third party to dissipate tensions and side-step issues between a dyad, or twosome. Triangulation can help satisfy the togetherness needs of duo's at the expense of a third party or ideology. In better-functioning family systems, alliances form flexibly so more needs are met over time. In rigid systems alliances become fixed, usually to the detriment of some members.

Dogs are certainly prime candidates to serve as legs in family triangles. For example, a wife was a dog's protector, the one who made sure his needs were faithfully met. The husband grumbled continually about the dog and refused to contribute to his care. One might assume the husband didn't like the dog and the feeling was mutual because the dog wanted nothing to do with the husband. However, when the wife was hospitalized, the husband and dog bonded and the husband tended lovingly to the dog's needs. When the wife came home, she picked up where she left off with the dog and the husband returned to complaining unremittingly about the dog, and again kept his distance. The triad returned to the old equilibrium.

In another arrangement, a young couple avoids dealing with their financial problems when they unite in concern for their anxious, fearful dog. If the dog's behavior issues were resolved, they would have to face up to money woes. As such, they only make headway with their dog after the husband is offered a promotion at work and a hefty raise.

Anxiety and Triangulation

Why do some families manage to work through their issues in reasonably straightforward ways, while others resort to triangulation that results in significant dysfunction? According to Dr. Murray Bowen, a psychiatrist and father of family systems theory, the higher the level of anxiety in a system, the greater the propensity to triangulate. Bowen likened the action in families to the movement of heated molecules. Anxiety is the "heat" that increases the activity of triangles.[103]

Let's examine Bowen's point through the following scenario:

Suppose a young married woman is extremely busy and her mother calls. Her mother discerns from background noise that the daughter is typing. The mother says, "I must have caught you at a bad time. Why don't I call back later? I'll let you get your work done." The mother's response doesn't cause the daughter to feel anxious. She responds, "No, I'll have even less time later and besides, I'm really interested and if you don't mind, I can multi task" or, "Can I call you back in a few days when I'm finished with my project?" The mother and daughter resolve the issue without creating an emotional drama over it.

Alternatively, suppose the mother calls, hears her daughter clicking away in

103   Guerin, Philip, Thomas Fogarty, Leo Fay, and Judith Kautto. *Working with Relationship Triangles: The One-Two-Three of Psychotherapy*. The Guilford Press: New York, 1996. P. 67-69

the background and asks in an accusatory way, "Are you typing?" The daughter responds, "Yes, I'm swamped with work." The mother answers with a long silence that seems to convey the daughter's choices are wrong and she should be giving the mother her full attention. The mother caps this off by saying, "I'm sorry I bothered you" and quickly gets off the phone. The daughter feels anxious, guilty for disappointing her mother, and angry with her mother for being insensitive to her needs (again). She finds it hard to concentrate on her work and worries that her mother will complain to her father and siblings (again) that she is rude and thoughtless. In short, the mother turned up the thermostat, got the "molecules" hopping, and, as a result, the daughter became, not more thoughtful, but more anxious and less productive. We might presume the same occurs with dogs: we can tone down and have a calming effect or ratchet things up and make our dogs more anxious.

In triangles, there are typically two insiders and an outsider. Leaders in family systems theory and therapy speculate that during periods of mild or moderate anxiety, outsiders long to belong and regret being isolated. However, when the tensions are heightened, it is usually preferable to be on the outside and free from the tension of anxious, conflicted "players."[104] If tensions are high over dog's issues, it might be time to call in a qualified professional, if one can be found.

....
104   Michael Kerr, M.D.. "Family Systems Theory and Therapy" in *Handbook of Family Therapy*. Edited by A. Gurman and D. Kniskern. Brunner/Muzel: New York, 1981. P. 241.

Finding Top Foods

It's epidemic in America: families are giving their dogs low caliber, processed foods and presumably expecting their health to hold. Some dog food companies are pouring huge amounts of money into advertising and giving free samples to veterinarians to pass along to their clients. This is occurring sometimes irrespective of the actual quality of the food.

A number of veterinarians have not studied nutrition and some are recommending the lower caliber foods to clients for their dogs and puppies and telling them, for example, "grocery store kibble is as satisfactory as the top brands". Clients might like to hear this because, in the short-term, it saves them money. However, it's not cost-effective if dogs experience more illnesses in their lifetimes and the veterinary costs are higher as a result.

Another advantage to high caliber foods is dogs need less of it to meet their nutritional needs. The output is smaller because less food is ingested and more retained.

Not all veterinarians are tone-deaf to dog's nutritional needs. It's possible that a strong majority have responsibly *self-educated* and completed continuing education in this area, though their learning may not have been measured. The bottom line, again, is that it can pay to do your own research on diet and other health-related issues to ensure that you understand which options are best.

You may have to experiment to find a high caliber food that's a good match for your dog's nutritional and digestive needs and taste preferences. Your veterinarian or a veterinary or canine nutritionist might help you, though outside the veterinary fields its caveat emptor. If your dog is eating non-nutritive substances, for example drywall, there might be micronutrient issues or a fiber deficit or other serious health issues that a veterinarian could diagnose.

The Web site, *Dog Food Analysis*, offers reliable information.[105] The *Whole Dog Journal* publishes annual lists of top-ranked dog foods accompanied by articles on their selection criteria.[106] Access is by subscription only though you can order individual articles for a fee. A "How to Choose the Right Dog Food" report is sometimes available for free on the *Whole Dog Journal* Web site.

I do come across dogs experiencing symptoms such as vomiting and diarrhea and when their families switch dog foods, some symptoms disappear. We had this with our own dogs. They both became sick at the same time. We switched from one high-rated food to a different, high-rated food and both immediately recovered. This occurred after the well-publicized, major food recalls. My experience suggests there are still problem ingredients in some foods; in addition, I know of recent recalls that aren't getting the same media attention as the earlier, massive recalls.

105   Dog Food Analysis, <http://www.dogfoodanalysis.com>.
106   Whole Dog Journal, <http://www.whole-dog-journal.com>.

Medicating Behavior

For information on psychotropic medications for dogs, written by known, reliable sources, visit the Web sites listed below. My inclusion of these articles should not be taken as an endorsement of everything written in them. We must approach the truth about psychotropic medications with respect for the complexity of the issues, and recognize our own limited understanding of them. Most of us would prefer drug-free solutions but blanket "no never" pronouncements will deal out some dogs that would benefit significantly from them.

Medicating Behavior Articles

- DVM360.com posts some excellent articles on the use of medications to treat behavior. One informative article by Dr. Karen Overall, a veterinary behaviorist, can be found there: "Your guide to understanding how behavior medications work", veterinarynews.dvm360.com/.

- Another useful article by Dr. Overall is, "Storm Phobias", *DVM Newsmagazine*, Sept 1, 2004. veterinarynews.dvm360.com/.

- WebMD posts a very comprehensive article to their Web site, "Treating Behavior Problems in Dogs" written by an ASPCA Virtual Pet Behaviorist, pets.webmd.com/dogs/guide/dog-be-havior-problems-medications/.

Every dog owner and veterinarian should read what Dr. Overall has to say about acepromazine in "Storm Phobias". Here's the essence of what she writes:

"…The common 'treatment' for storm and noise phobias and veterinary office visits is acepromazine. In truth, I wish this medication would be placed at the far back of a top shelf and used only exceptionally. Acepromazine is a dissociative anesthetic meaning that it scrambles perceptions… and we make many if not most dogs more sensitive to storms by using this drug."[107]

Again, in my opinion it's inhumane to expect veterinarians to know all the relevant medical facts about every species they work with and every drug they administer, including psychotropic medications. It's too much. Why not find your own information about behavior problems and associated medical conditions? Unlike veterinarians, families have to become experts only on the companion animal they have. They don't have to be a "Whisperer" or have special gifts to understand what is reinforcing their dog's behavior, and they don't have to go to veterinary school to research information that sheds light on their dog's problems. My advice is the same for humans attempting to navigate the health care system: find reliable sources of information so you can assist in your own care. Take responsibility. Don't leave it all to your medical doctors or veterinarians.

107   Karen L. Overall, VMD, PhD, Dipl. ACVB. "Storm Phobias", *DVM Newsmagazine*, Sept 1, 2004. <http://www.veterinarynews.dvm360.com/>

Music for Calm

Studies show that soothing music can lower heart rates, pulse, blood pressure and respirations, affect brain activity, reduce anxiety and stress, with other benefits. Research on the effect of music made for dogs is referenced on the *Through a Dog's Ear* Web site.[108]

I often recommend music to help dogs relax. The music can also be used to calm large groups of dogs in kennels and shelters. My cost-conscious clients ask, can't they just play "Amazing Grace" or something similar that they have on-hand. I say, sure, give it a try. However, calming music made especially for dogs can be purchased on the Internet, at the locations listed below, and it is designed to have a more beneficial effect than music picked randomly.

My clients report success with music and they love having this option because it's natural and risk-free. The worst it can do is put you to sleep too. Unlike humans, dogs don't need variety. I don't know of a single dog that grew sick of beautiful sounds because the music was played too often. Do you?

Music for Dogs

- Pet Pause—Harp music by Sue Raimond on CDs, www.pet-pause2000.com/

- Through a Dog's Ear, throughadogsear.com/

- Canine Lullabies, caninelullabies.com/

- Laughing Dog, www.petalk.org/LaughingDog.html

---

108 Through a Dog's Ear, <http://www.throughadogsear.com/research.htm>.

Muzzles

 Notwithstanding the effect on the victim, one of the worst things that can happen to a dogs is to have him or her bite humans, even if the bites were obviously provoked by humans. To make my point, I'll recount three scenarios for you concerning dogs that delivered puncture wounds:

One: A Doberman pinscher is tied to the interior of his family's boat. A new dock neighbor stops by to introduce herself. Not seeing the owners, she whisks past the "beware of dog" sign and clambers aboard the boat. The dog barks, growls, and finally lunges and bites her. The dog's family pays her doctor's bill and the woman develops a phobia of dogs. She doesn't apologize for her role in the debacle. She says she didn't know their dog was "vicious".

Two: A Golden retriever is sitting in the car while his humans finish shopping. A passer-by who loves Golden's sidles up to the window to say "Hello". When the Golden shrinks back, she sticks her hand in. He bites her. She apologizes for provoking him and goes off to nurse her wounds.

Unfortunately, when aggression is used successfully, i.e., from an anxious dog's perspective, if he bites and succeeds in driving away the objects of his fears and confusion, the next time he feels anxious and confused we can presume he will bite again. Dogs do what works for them.

Three: A German shepherd mix is allowed to attend a small party. She is anxious around strangers, has snapped at them, but has not bitten. A quiet, dog-savvy seven-year-old, who has played successfully with the dog in the past, stops to pet her. The dog tolerates the petting well. However, when the mother sees the child with the dog she screams in alarm and jumps in to separate her child from the dog, who then lunges at the mother and bites her; the mother requires stitches. As it happens, the dog is sound sensitive and she may have thought the mother wanted to hurt her and the child. The mother sues the family and wants the dog declared dangerous and euthanized. At this point I will posit that competent dog people are calm, not given to hysterics.

If these three dogs were wearing muzzles, they would have been protected from the three humans who did not use the best judgment, and the humans would have been protected from dogs that did not have the ability to differentiate reliably between friend and foe (and fool).

Dogs that bite are difficult to rehome and, as mentioned previously, many rescue organizations refuse to take in dogs with bite histories. In addition, dogs quickly develop the habit of biting if they are successful at it. Woe to the dog that discovers biting as a satisfying way to deal with his anxieties, fears and innate drives.

I support the use of muzzles if they can be introduced properly and if muzzling the dog does not lead to increased aggression when the dog is not muzzled. As always, we watch for feedback from our dogs. They let us know if our interventions fit. This is an area where direction from a qualified, competent behavior professional who knows your dog would be especially helpful.

The biggest problem I see with muzzles is that families don't take the time to acclimate their dogs to them before they have to be applied as emergency measures to prevent biting, for example, in a veterinarian's office or when visitors are milling about. Families could expand their reactive dog's possibilities if they adapted them to muzzles early on, before they run into situations where they become an essential tool.

There's the question of course, when is use of a muzzle justified? There's so much variability among biting dogs. When my Yorkie, Piper, used to "bite", he would make a lot of noise but just graze the skin surface and not leave any mark. It was quick and it felt as if someone was brushing a finger over our hands. When he came to us as a puppy at twelve weeks I taught him to inhibit his bites, using the protocol originated by Dr. Ian Dunbar (see "Puppy Tips" in this section). Before me, his breeder similarly taught him valuable lessons about bite inhibition.

Piper likes to guard precious resources. He also gets irritated, or reactive, for example, if I spend too much time clipping his nails or a family member other than me tries to take valued bones from him, though he's become a lot more tolerant over the years. I wouldn't of course use a muzzle with him. If a dog has a harder mouth and leaves marks or punctures skin, and the dog has to be around people or animals that might trigger the aggression, I would acclimate the dog to muzzling so I could use one, if necessary, as a protective measure for all participants including the dog.

Families with biting dogs can be reluctant to have their dogs seen in muzzles. What will the neighbors think? Indeed, many humans do have biases, especially if their own dogs don't need a muzzle. Don't let competitive or critical neighbors, friends, and relatives get the best of you: do what's right and best for your dog and others. If you hold your ground, critical observers might change their point of view.

Muzzles can be used for other protective purposes. For example, some families put muzzles on their separation anxious dogs when they go out so the dogs can't trash the house or hurt their teeth and gums gnawing on wood and other surfaces and objects. I don't recommend leaving muzzles on dogs when they can't be supervised. However, what are families to do if we tell them their potential solutions are all too risky? Too risky for whom? If families can't solve their problems with dogs, dogs are apt to suffer end-of-the-line outcomes. I know of families that have successfully muzzled their separation anxious dogs for up to three hours, after getting their dogs used to muzzles over several weeks. I don't know of a client family that used muzzling as an all-day strategy while they went off to work or school. If the dog is so distressed that it needs a muzzle to stay home alone, other treatment is desperately needed, such as medications prescribed by a veterinarian and a behavior modification plan. If you have a separation anxious dog it would be wise, at a minimum, to get your dog used to wearing a muzzle just in case it's ever needed, as part of an emergency management strategy.

If you introduce a muzzle properly and the dog is still upset by it, consider that you may not ever be able to use a muzzle on that dog. And so it is with all interventions we try on our dogs.

I want to be clear about two points: I would not use a muzzle on a dog for management without also working to modify behaviors and get problems from different angles. In addition, I would not ever leave a muzzled dog unsupervised. However, I am very slow to criticize families with limited options for doing what they must to keep loved dogs with their families.

Finding a Muzzle

First, find a comfortable muzzle that fits. You can buy by breed and head shape using your dog's head measurements. You can look for a suitable muzzle in a pet store but Internet sources are apt to offer a wider variety at better prices (I list two sources below). Think about what you want to accomplish with the muzzle and what type of muzzles will meet your dog's needs.

Nylon Muzzle: If you want a muzzle you can slip on and off for quick procedures such as nail clipping and examinations by veterinarians, a nylon muzzle might be best. They're inexpensive, soft, easy to cart around, and sold in most pet stores. Acclimate your dog to the muzzle long before you need it.

Basket and Leather Muzzles: If you anticipate your dog will have to wear a muzzle for long stretches of time, for example, when you have visitors, consider the wire basket or leather muzzle. Make sure they are shaped so your dog can open his mouth to pant, drink water, and accept small treats.

The better option for many dogs is to confine them to an out-of-the-way place in the house where there are no visitors to contend with. (See the section on "Murphy" to help you assess if excluding the dog would help or hinder progress.) You can't use confinement, or ostracism, or muzzling, if the result is increased agitation and aggression. On the other hand, if you have not made it worth your dog's while to adjust to a muzzle, he will likely reject it.

The oft-cited drawback to muzzles is that head-banging dogs may try to hit their "enemies" with them as a substitute for biting. If your dog doesn't use his head as a weapon, a basket muzzle or leather muzzle may be satisfactory for longer-term, supervised wear.

Protocol for Introducing a Muzzle

Show your dog the muzzle in a quiet, relaxed setting. If your dog is already acclimated to relaxing to soothing music, play the music for a few minutes before introducing the muzzle. Let your dog sniff to investigate. Be cheerful, as if the muzzle is a fun toy. Give him (or her) treats when he approaches it. Put treats in the muzzle so he has to touch the muzzle to get the treats. Put the muzzle away. Repeat this procedure over and over —you want him to build a positive association to the muzzle. Easy does it! You can build a more solid foundation for muzzle wear if you move slowly through this phase.

Gradually expect more from your dog when you introduce the muzzle. Keep playing the music in a relaxed setting. Have especially high-value treats in view, for example, the Super-Motivating treats. Touch the muzzle to your dog's face and give him a treat. Eventually, slip the muzzle on your dog without fastening it and reward him by taking it off without delay. Slowly increase the time you leave it on from a fraction of a second to a few seconds to minutes. Instead of rewarding him every time, reward him only for the times he remains still. Continue doing this without forcing the muzzle on him.

Finally fasten the muzzle and leave it on for longer periods: When he's relaxed with the muzzle, fasten it and leave it on for a short time, less than a minute. Gradually increase the length of time you leave it on. Give him high-value treats when the muzzle's on and when you take it off. Work up to leaving the muzzle on for increasingly long periods of time. Reward him at intervals if he's relaxed about the muzzle. Don't let him get to the point where he's agitated about the muzzle, at any point during the process.

Vary settings: When he's relaxed in a muzzle you can use it for short car rides and walks but still avoid situations that would cause him to be agitated. Reinforce him with treats and happy talk when you take the muzzle off.

Ready for purposeful use: When the above routine is established you can muzzle him when you encounter a situation that's apt to trigger an aggressive response and you aren't sure you can supervise as fully as might be necessary.

Where to Find Muzzles

You might find a muzzle locally at a pet store or on the Internet. There are a number of companies that sell muzzles on the Internet. I have clients that have ordered successfully from the following online shops:

- Pet Expertise
  www.petexpertise.com/dog-training-aids/jafco-muzzles

- Morrco Pet Supply
  www.morrco.com/dogmuzzles1.html

Puppy Tips

Prevention is best. Dr. Ian Dunbar, one of the foremost dog trainers in the world, posted an invaluable article to the Inernet, no cost, called "Before You Get Your Puppy".[109] Dr. Dunbar introduced lure and reward methods of training that are consistent with the simple interventions set forth in this book. The Dog Star Daily Web site posts additional useful, reliable information on puppy and dog training, with some behavior advice. I also recommend that you peruse articles on the Clicker Solutions Web site, www.clickersolutions.com/articles.

If families get things right from the beginning, dogs prone to be more anxious or aggressive can learn to live in harmony with us in spite of their reactivity.

If you see early signs of "temperament" in a puppy— for example, resource guarding or behavior on the high end of excitability, understand that you will have to go extra miles to get a reliable dog that won't present later with deal-breaking issues.

Before and After You Get Your Puppy

- Dog Star Daily, www.dogstardaily.com/training/you-get-your-puppy, or James & Kenneth Publishers, http://stores.lulu.com/dogstardaily

- Video by Ian Dunbar: *SIRIUS Puppy Training REDUX*. DVD. James & Kenneth Publishers. 2008. Sample clips can be viewed and videos purchased at www.dogwise.com.

109   Ian Dunbar, DVM. *Before You Get Your Puppy*, <http:// www.dogstardaily.com/training/you-get-your-puppy>.

Stimulating Environments

I am surprised sometimes by all that families do to ensure their pet's lives are tidy and orderly. It's true, dogs typically respond well, as we do, to routine, but why do so much for them if it deprives them of entertainment and the fun of doing for themselves?

For starters, if we have to feed our dogs, usually twice daily plus treats, and dogs are natural scavengers, why give it to them in the same bowl every day when we could scatter their dry food in a designated indoor spot or on a solid outdoor surface and let them "find" the pieces? Or why not fill a Buster cube or other interactive toys with a mix of dry food and treats and let our dogs spend time trying to get pieces out? As another alternative, put a mix of dry food, treats and a touch of peanut butter in a Kong, freeze it, and leave it out for your dog while you go shopping or to work. (If you visit www.kong-company.com/worlds_best.html/ on the Internet you'll find Kong recipes, everything from "Banana Rama" to "Cheesy Delights" and "Kong on a Rope".)

If your dog is naughty, hyperactive or destructive, you can use food as a reinforcer to woo him away from bad habits, as illustrated throughout this book. When there's a need for so much behavior modification, why not put the food bowl away for the duration so you can use every scrap to change behavior?

Taking this further, have you tried hiding dry food and treats in an old towel, sock, or cardboard box? In addition, put water in a child-size small pool and float cut-up vegetables in it, such as carrots and celery. Some dogs will need a few days to discover that such play is fun.

If your dog likes to dig, read the section in Behavior Cache on how to create a dig box or space in your yard.

Hang inner tubes or old tires and attach ropes so your dog can pull on them for entertainment.

See if there are tracking, flyball or agility classes in your community. You and your dog might enjoy one of these sports. As described in Section One, dogs that have developed tracking abilities can serve usefully in their communities.

The absolute most popular toy with my clients has been the interactive Chase 'N Pull Toy by Vee Enterprises, carried by the reputable Dogwise.[110] Dogs may give up on chasing cars or other moving objects if they are prevented from chasing because they are on-leash, and when they see a car coming, their attention is diverted to the Chase 'N Pull Toy instead.

Michelle Douglas[111] is a dog trainer and behavior consultant in West Haven, Connecticut and the current president of the Association of Pet Dog Trainers.[112] She shared the following story with me, one of many that affirms there is a unique role for qualified trainers in the modification and management of behavior problems.

As we know, some dogs aren't happy unless they have a job. Michelle's client was an Australian shepherd that was going a bit stir crazy in his house. With nothing else to do with his time, he would herd the children. Michelle taught the family to teach him to gather dirty laundry from the bedrooms and put it in piles next to the clothes hamper. After that, when he tried to herd the children, they diverted him to gathering dirty clothes. In the autumn when he was on his own in the yard, he expanded his job to herding the fallen leaves into piles. We can surmise this Australian Shepherd was the only dog in his community to become known for his skills at herding leaves! I wonder if he has become the envy of his neighborhood.

....

110   Dogwise, <http://www.dogwise.com>.
111   Michelle Douglas, Refined Canine, <http://www.refinedcanine.com>.
112   Association of Pet Dog Trainers, <http://www.apdt.com>.

Stress

Some families are surprised when I tell them, "Wow, your dog is really stressed". They want to know, how can I tell. It's instructive for me: humans can look and not see. This happens especially with busy parents whose dogs are obviously (to me) stressed by young children.

In another scenario, families conclude their dogs have dominance issues when the dogs are actually having difficulty coping with their environments.

Dog's families are told to socialize, socialize, socialize their puppies before the critical age of three months. However, what puppies need most is *successful* socialization. As such, I recommend they be removed from any setting if they are showing more than minimal signs of stress. What good does it do if their early experiences with people, dogs and other animals are not confidence-building?

Signs of Stress

- SALIVATING AND PANTING

- PACING

- LIP-LICKING

- SNEEZING

- TREMBLING

- WHINING

- DILATED PUPILS

- URINATING AT THE WRONG TIMES

- Diarrhea or precipitous bowel movements

- Growling

- Nipping

- Shedding

- Coughing

- Scratching or licking excessively

- Avoiding eye contact, turning head away

- Hiding behind furniture, humans, etc.

A valuable article, "The Neurological and Pharmacological Basis for Fears and Anxieties", written by Dr. Debra Horwitz, a veterinary behaviorist in St. Louis, Missouri and president of the American College of Veterinary Behaviorists, is available on the Internet.[113] She states, "Stress has long been thought to have metabolic effects and behavioral effects. When using the term stress when applied to humans and animals we are normally describing a situation where the environmental situations are having an adverse effect on the individual. Often stress is difficult to quantify for companion animals, but most of us would agree that it can be a factor in behavioral disorders in companion animals.[114]

I suspect that much of the environmental stress on dogs comes from humans who think their dogs are trying to dominate so they must be dominated in return. The dogs are usually just trying to get basic needs met. If they hog food it's because they want more of it and perhaps they are naturally prone to guarding resources. If they go flying out the door ahead of us, they want to get to the other side, especially if the door leads outdoors and it appears you are going out there with them. There are a myriad of reasons dogs do things. One of the least likely and overused explanations is they are trying to rule the roost.

....

113   Debra Horwitz, DVM, DACVB. "The Neurological and Pharmacological Basis for Fears and Anxieties". *Atlantic Coast Veterinary Conference*, 2001. <http://vetmedicine.about.com>. For access to the full article, type the article's title in the search box.

114   Ibid.

Super-Motivating Treats

For most dogs, Chicken Meatballs make the perfect Super-Motivating treat. I use the term super-motivating because they are so appealing that the dogs easily give up other pursuits and engage in trying to get more of them. The recipe and instructions are below. Check with your veterinarian if you have questions about ingredients, and proceed with caution if your dog has known food allergies.

Recipe for Chicken Meatballs

1 Chicken breast, cooked and cut or shredded in small pieces

1 TBSP mild, shredded cheddar cheese

1 cup white rice, cooked

Dry dog food or treats, 1/2 to 1 cup

1 to 2 raw eggs

Garlic powder, a dash or two

Preheat oven to 350 degrees. Combine all ingredients. Form mix into meatballs, 1" to 1 ½". Apply cooking spray. Meatballs can be placed close together. Cook for 20 minutes or so.

Introducing Super-Motivating Treats

The instructions are approximately as follows:

First assemble the ingredients. Interest your dog in what you are doing. Attach a name to the meatballs, for example, "Chickies" (use hard sounds). Be fun; use a high-pitched voice and squeaky toy as you mix ingredients. Let your dog sniff the bowl. Let him/her sniff the oven-ready sheet with meatballs on it. Make a big splash about putting Chickies in the oven and removing them from the oven.

When Chickies are cool enough, give your dog a couple of little pieces. Say, "Do you want a Chickie?" Your goal is to condition your dog to become excited and very interested in your treats so his interest in the treats trump his interest in triggers (such as visitors, neighbors, animals, etc.).

After baking, freeze some on a baking sheet (so they don't stick together) and when frozen, place them in a freezer bag. You can pretend to hide some in a drawer and then bring them out after a few seconds or longer to build maximum interest. If you have your dog's rapt attention you can create more excitement if you leave them in the drawer longer; if your dog's attention fades as soon as the Chickies are out of sight, bring them out quickly. If your dog becomes over-the-top excited and starts engaging in unwanted behaviors, skip putting them in the drawer. As always, listen to your dog to discover what movements he enjoys.

You will use these treats only to modify the more challenging behaviors. Save them for what matters most.

If your dog has apprehensions about visitors, cook the Chickies shortly before visitors arrive so your dog is really tuned in and excited about the Chickies and trying to figure out how to get some from you. After you have done this a few times your dog will be expecting Chickies when company arrives and you will be able to take some from the freezer and defrost some in time for company. For the first few times, or as long as it is making a difference, bake them on the spot.

To build your dog's interest in the Super-Motivating treats, say fun things like "Where's Chickies?" , "Where'd Chickie go?" Skip, dance, act goofy. If you've hidden a few Chickies in a drawer, slowly open the door with drama and fun. Grab the Chickies and run to another room with them with your dog hopefully following. If your dog isn't interested, or is put off, or overwhelmed by your antics, skip this (zany fun) part.

Use your squeaky toy to announce a Chickie is on its way.

Pretend to eat some yourself.

After you're successful with the initial training, your dog should only get small chunks from Chickies as bonuses, or when you want to encourage a very important new behavior. For some dogs this might mean they will learn to let go of their interest in people, dogs, or other triggers, and to tune in to the Chickie (and other reinforcers such as a squeaky toy or a Kong with small amounts of peanut butter on it to lick, or opportunities to chase a ball) instead.

Do not give dogs verbal corrections for anything they might do when they are being reinforced with Chickies. This is not like obedience training. We want it to be a pure joy for your dog to let go of an interest that sparks reactivity, and redirect to the Chickies.

Bibliography

Aloff, Brenda. *Aggression in Dogs: Practical Management Prevention and Behaviour Modification*. Dogwise Publishing, 2001.

AVSAB Position Statement, "The Use of Punishment for Behavior Modification in Animals". American Veterinary Society of Animal Behavior. http://www.avsabonline.org.

Bailey, Jon S. PhD, Burch, Mary, PhD. *How to Think Like a Behavior Analyst*. Lawrence Erlbaum Assoc Inc, 2006.

Beaver, Bonnie, BS, DVM, MS, DACVB. *Canine Behavior: A Guide for Veterinarians*. W.B. Saunders Company, 1999.

Boneham, Sheila Webster, PhD. *Rescue Matters: How to Find, Foster, and Rehome Companion Animals*. Thorndike Press, 2009.

Burch, Mary PhD and Jon S. Bailey PhD. *How Dogs Learn*, Howell Book House, 1999.

Campbell, WE. "Which dog breeds develop what behavioral problems?" *Modern Veterinary Practice*. 1972: 53:31.

Case, Linda P.. *The Dog: Its Behavior, Nutrition, and Health*. Blackwell Publishing ltd., 2nd ed., 2005.

DeNapoli JS., Dodman NH., et al. "Effect of dietary protein content and tryptophan supplementation on dominance aggression, territorial aggression, and hyperactivity in dogs." *Journal of the American Veterinary Medical Association*, 217(4), (Aug 15, 2000):504-08.

Dodman, NH, Karlsson, EK, et al. "A canine chromosome 7 locus confers compulsive disorder susceptibility." *Molecular Psychiatry*. 15 (2010): 8–10; doi:10.1038/mp.2009.111.

Dunbar, Ian, DVM, PhD, MRCVS. "Housetraining: Solve the Problem by Understanding the Process." http://www.billfoundation.org/html/housetraining.html.

Flannigan, G., DVM, MSc and Dodman, N.H., BVMS, DACVB. "Risk Factors and Behaviors Associated with Separation Anxiety in Dogs". *Journal of the American Veterinary Medical Association*, 219(4) (Aug 15, 2001): 460-66.

Frank, Diane, DVM, DACVB, B. Beauchamp, PhD, C. Palestrini, DVM, PhD. "Systematic review of the use of pheromones for treatment of undesirable behavior in cats and dogs. J. of American Veterinary Medical Association. June 15, 2010, Vol. 236, No. 12, p. 1308-1316.

Frankl, Viktor, MD. *Man's Search for Meaning*. New York: Washington Square Press, Simon and Schuster, 1963, 127.

Grandin, Temple, PhD and Catherine Johnson, PhD. *Animals Make Us Human: Creating the Best Life for Animals*. Mariner Books, 2010.

Guerin, Philip, T. Fogarty and J. Kautto. *Working with Relationship Triangles: The One-Two-Three of Psychotherapy*. The Guildford Press: New York, 1996. P. 67-69.

Kerr, Michael, MD. "Family Systems Theory and Therapy" in *Handbook of Family Therapy*, edited by A. Gurman and D. Kniskern. Brunner/Muzel: New York, 1981. P. 241.

Lindsay, Steven and Victoria Lea Voith. *Applied Dog Behavior and Training, Volume 1: Adaptation and Learning*. Blackwell Publishing, 2000.

Lindsay, Steven. *Handbook of Applied Dog Behavior and Training, Volume 3: Procedures and Protocols*. Blackwell Publishing, 2005.

McCrave, E.A. "Diagnostic criteria of separation anxiety in the dog." *Veterinary Clinics of North America, Small Animal Practice*, 21(2) (1991): 247-55.

McDevitt, Leslie. *Control Unleashed: Creating a Focused and Confident Dog*. Clean Run Productions, 2007.

Minuchin, Salvador, MD *Family Healing: Strategies for Hope and Understanding*. Free Press, 1998.

Morris, Charles. *Psychology: An Introduction*. Prentice Hall. 7th ed., 1990.

Muller-Schwarze, Dietland, and Robert M Silverstein, eds. *Chemical Signals in Vertebrates*. New York: Plenum Press, 1977. 455-64.

Overall, Karen, VMD. *Clinical Behavioral Medicine for Small Animals.* Mosby, 1997.

Overall, Karen, VMD, PhD, Dipl. ACVB. "Storm Phobias". *DVM Newsmagazine*, Sept 1. 2004. http://www.veterinarynews.dvm360.com/.

Rosales-Ruiz, PhD, Kellie Snider, MS. Constructional Aggression Treatment: Shaping Your Way Out of Aggression. Tawzer Dog Videos, DVDs. 2nd Ed., 2010.

Salman MD, Hutchinson J, Ruch-Gallie R, et al. "Behavioral Reasons for Relinquishment of Dogs and Cats to 12 Shelters." *Journal of Applied Animal Welfare Science*, 3 (2000): 93-106.

Schoon, A. "The Performance of Dogs in Identifying Humans by Scent." (PhD dissertation, Rijksuniveristeit, Leiden), 1997.

Scott, John Paul and John L. Fuller. *Genetics and the Social Behavior of the Dog.* Chicago: University of Chicago Press, 1965.

Spector, Morgan. "Moving Beyond the Dominance Myth: Toward an Understanding of Training as Partnership", 2001.

Szetei, V., Miklosi, A., Topal, J., Csanyi, V. "When dogs seem to lose their nose: an investigation on the use of visual and olfactory cues in communicative context between dog and owner." *Applied Animal Behavior Science*, 83 (2003): 141-152.

Task Force on General Education (TFGE). General Education Gains. Harvard Magazine. (January 2, 2007). http://www.fas.harvard.edu/~secfas/Gen_Ed_Prelim_Report.htm.

Vaillant, George MD. *Spiritual Evolution: A Scientific Defense of Faith.* Broadway Books, 2008.

Voith VL, Borchelt PL. "Separation anxiety in dogs." *The Compendium on Continuing Education for the Practicing Veterinarian* 7(1) (1985): 42.

Voith VL and Ganster D. "Separation anxiety: Review of 42 cases." *Applied Animal Behavior Science,* 37 (1993): 84-85.

Yin, Sophia, DVM, MS. "New Study Finds Popular "Alpha Dog" Training Techniques Can Cause More Harm Than Good." <http://www.askdryin.com> March 9, 2009

"We need another and a wiser and perhaps a more mystical concept of animals. … We patronize them for their incompleteness, for their tragic fate for having taken form so far below ourselves. And therein do we err. For the animal shall not be measured by man. In a world older and more complete than ours, they move finished and complete, gifted with the extension of the senses we have lost or never attained, living by voices we shall never hear. They are not brethren, they are not underlings: they are other nations, caught with ourselves in the net of life and time, fellow prisoners of the splendour and travail of the earth."

~ Henry Beston, Author of *The Outermost House*

Index

P

Pain, 33, 58, 142, 183, 186
Partnership, 193
Pathology, 191
Patrolling, 154, 156
Pattern, 28, 44-45, 82, 84, 154, 156
Patterns of reinforcement, 37, 154
Pee, 24, 37, 99-101, 108, 111
People-friendly, 49
Pet sitters, 71
Phobia, 203
Physiology, 166
Pica, 15, 165
Pit bull, 182
Play, 38, 72, 82, 100, 125, 127-128,
    152, 193, 202, 207
Portuguese water dog, 29
Positive regard, 50-52, 54, 59, 73
Positive reinforcement training, 43,
    47, 193
Possessive aggression, 159
Praise, 112, 185, 191
Predators, 154, 156, 159
Pre-departure cues, 126-128
Priorities, 30
Profession, 27, 31, 57, 59, 61, 62, 65,
    69, 73
Professionalism, 52, 59, 62-64, 69,
Projection, 50, 54, 56, 59
Prong collar, 53
Protein, 104, 168-169
Protocols, 91, 95, 124, 130, 160, 167-
    169, 177-178, 204
Psychiatrist, 53, 196
Psychologists, 26, 68, 185
Psychology, 35, 64, 66-67, 135
Psychosomatic, 35
Psychotherapy, 63, 68
Psychotropic, 90
Punish, 36, 50, 103, 128, 133, 143,
    159
Punishment, 41, 45-47, 69, 81, 91, 97,
    123, 141-142, 179-180, 185
PupGear Corporation, 106
Pup-Grass, 106-107
Pup-Head, 108
Puppies, 29, 55-56, 80-82, 84-85, 97,
    100, 103, 107, 135, 152-153,
    144, 171, 198, 204, 209, 212
Puppy Kindergarten 83-84

Q

Qualifying exams, 67

R

Rain, 38, 98, 109
Reactivity, 48, 90-92, 126, 145, 169,
    209, 216
Rehome, 123-124
Reinforcers, 28, 36-39, 47, 91-92,
    104, 107, 111, 129-130, 147,
    158, 160, 216
Relationships, 41, 43-44, 47, 61, 67,
    72, 115, 117-118, 189
Remote training collar, 153
Rescue, 19, 21, 23, 41, 70, 80, 97,
    131, 133, 138, 187, 198
Research, 29, 43, 56, 59, 62, 65-67,
    71-73, 99, 135, 166, 169, 198,
    201-202
Resource guarding, 159, 209
Resources, 28, 30-31, 68, 116, 136,
    158-159, 181, 205, 213
Respect, 6, 29, 48, 51, 54, 66, 71, 96,
    154, 168, 192, 200
Rewards, 24, 39, 43, 47-48, 91-93,
    104, 106, 111, 129-130, 149,
    158, 180
Risk, 29, 47, 79, 104, 117, 122, 123,
    133, 140, 156, 202

About the Author

Lynn Hoover is an expert in dog behavior problems and family relationships, interviewing and systems consulting—and a leading authority on the profession of dog behavior consulting. She founded the International Association of Animal Behavior Consultants and founded and served as Chair of their Dog division for four years. She is a long-time advocate for standards and meaningful certification.

Lynn is a medical family therapist with long-standing eligibility for Clinical membership in the American Association for Marriage and Family Therapy. She is the author of *Dog Quirks And Behavior Solutions* and a text, *The Family in Dog Behavior Consulting*. She has a private behavior consulting practice in Pittsburgh, Pennsylvania.